MY STO

My Story

by
PETER O'LEARY

A translation of the famous Irish classic
by
CYRIL Ó CÉIRÍN

Oxford   New York

OXFORD UNIVERSITY PRESS

1987

Oxford University Press, Walton Street, Oxford OX2 6DP

Oxford New York Toronto
Delhi Bombay Calcutta Madras Karachi
Petaling Jaya Singapore Hong Kong Tokyo
Nairobi Dar es Salaam Cape Town
Melbourne Auckland
and associated companies in
Beirut Berlin Ibadan Nicosia

Oxford is a trade mark of Oxford University Press

First published 1970 by Mercier Press
First issued, with a new introduction, as an Oxford University Press
paperback 1987

British Library Cataloguing in Publication Data
O'Leary, Peter
My story.
1. Ireland—Social life and customs—
19th century   2. Ireland—social life
and customs—20th century
I. Title   II. Céirín, Cyril T. Ó.   III. Mo
scéal féin. English
941.508'092'4   DA950.1
ISBN 0–19–282053–2

Library of Congress Cataloguing in Publication Data
O'Leary, Peter, 1839–1920.
My story.
Translation of: Mo Scéal Féin.
1. O'Leary, Peter, 1839–1920. 2. Catholic Church—
Ireland—Clergy—Biography. 3. Ireland—Social
conditions.   I. Title.
BX4705.0475A3 1987 282'.092'4 [B] 87–15394
ISBN 0–19–282053–2 (pbk.)

Printed in Great Britain by
The Guernsey Press Co. Ltd.
Guernsey, Channel Islands

To Kit

'Do chum glóire Dé is onóra na hÉireann'

ACKNOWLEDGEMENTS

I am very grateful to the Jesuit community at Mungret College, Limerick, for making the college libraries available to me; and especially to Fr Senan Timomey, S.J., Rector, both for his interest and for his suggested changes in the typescript; to the late Fr John A. Deevy, S.J., who sought out the information on Fr Terence Sheely, S.J., for me.

My thanks also to Cormac O'Connor, founder of Limerick's School of Adult Education, for reading the typescript.

In the past, scholars of the Irish language and literature were notorious for jealously keeping the fruits of their researches to themselves; fortunately, the same cannot be said of today's scholars. I thank the ever-generous Professor Brian Ó Cuív, Dublin Institute for Advanced Studies, for permission to use material of his in Appendix 14 and I acknowledge my debt to him in matters appertaining to the state of the Irish language since 1800—no study of the period can afford to ignore his work in this field.

I am also indebted to the equally kind Fr Tomás Ó Fiaich, Professor of Modern History at Maynooth, for information on the Church and Fenianism (Appendix 12) and for his suggestions as to further sources.

I thank Fr Peter Troddyn, S.J., for permission to quote Dr Douglas Hyde (from *Studies*) and also Fr James Stephenson, S.J., for permission to quote from *Irish Jesuit Directory and Yearbook*. Thanks also to Mainchín Seoighe for his assistance in some geographical problems and to those girls on the staff of the Limerick County Library who went to endless trouble on my behalf.

And finally, I am indebted to my wife, Kit, who was reader, editor, adviser and inspirer, all rolled into one.

Tá mé fíor-bhuíoch de na daoine seo thuas luaite.

C. Ó Céirín.

CONTENTS

INTRODUCTION

Canon Peter O'Leary, or An tAthair Peadar ('Father Peter') as he always was—and still is—colloquially known, wrote his own story, *Mo Scéal Féin*, in his native Gaelic in 1915. The first autobiography in modern Irish, it was written by the man of whom a contemporary, speaking for the Irish-Ireland revival movement as a whole, said that he was 'a little god to us all'. It still excites our interest today because it was an attempt at an ultimate declaration and apologia (almost, it might be said, a last will and testament) by one of the key-figures in the emergence of the Irish people to nationhood, being, as he was, both cultural and social reformer, Gaelic revival activist non-pareil, author and lecturer, and, indeed, polemic.

O'Leary's eighty-one year lifespan alone makes him a unique chronicler: he was born at the advent of the Great Hunger, a decade after the death of Raifteirí an File, the last well-known poet in the full Gaelic tradition; and he died on the eve of the founding of the Free State, within a decade of the birth of Brendan Behan, whose work may be said to have signalled the latest stage of Irish literature in the English language. This 'story' links the era of O'Connell with that of Collins. of Irish-speaking Ireland with the English-speaking, of near-slavery with near-independence, of William Carleton with James Joyce.

My Story is indeed a repository of palpable social history and (although to a less tangible degree) of political history, but its true value resides in the spirit in which it was conceived and by which it is informed and unified. Typically, An tAthair Peadar had little time for any soulless recording of events and consequences: for him the interpretation of history was always subjective. People, not histories, were his concern—*the* people, *a* people, and always as befitted a priest and a leader with his aristocratic ancestry, *his* people. Here is no dry-as-dust pedant, but a man who is wonderfully and sometimes exacerbatingly human. Because of his humanity, again and again one word crops up: *muintir*. Fr Dineen's famous dictionary gives us as English equivalents 'household, family, community, religious order, tribe, party, followers, residents, members, tenants, people, folk'. This placing of the 'people' at the centre of things was very much a Gaelic characteristic and the language itself indicates this readily. For example, in O'Leary's day, a close blood-relation might be distinguished by placing the word *dearbh* ('true') in conjunction with *muintir*; such terminology surely is illustrative of how closely knit were the rural communities he had experienced and wished to keep alive.

Elsewhere in this book I have indicated the importance of places and their names for one who was in the mainstream of Gaelic tradition. The reader may be struck by An tAthair Peadar's litanies of place-names; we can imagine him lovingly musing over them as an old mother, sitting alone by the open hearth, might murmur the names of her children. Often, too, he is at pains to explain or hazard a guess at the meaning of such names, attempting somewhat obviously to instil an awareness of roots (in both appropriate senses of the word!) into a generation fast losing them. The uninitiated might understand his attitude better if they knew that it was even not uncommon in olden days to stress the word *muintir* in place-names. The structure of Gaelic society was such, and there was so strong a bond between a 'people' and their land, that it was quite natural to refer to an area where, say, the Dineens predominated as *Muintir Dhuinnín*, the word for 'people' being used in place of 'landhold' or 'country'. O'Leary himself was born in the heart of the ancient territory of IveLeary or *Uíbh Laoghaire*, which means something like '(that which belongs) to the people of Laoghaire', his eponymous ancestor. Roots such as these he could never forget, and he felt that the Irish people as a whole would suffer an incalculable loss if allowed to lose touch with their own.

Indeed, it was his faith in the *muintir* that led to O'Leary's greatest contribution to the movement to restore the Irish language. Concerned as he was with the people, he was mainly interested in 'the living language in the mouths of people', when others, often with a Victorian sense of correctitude, were placing the emphasis on one kind of 'literary' Irish or another. In the words of Dr Douglas Hyde (*Studies*, June 1920):

Canon O'Leary's great merit is that he utterly turned his back upon everything that was bookish and old and unclear, and turned his face resolutely towards the folk speech of his native County Cork, which he wrote with a crystal clearness which has never been surpassed. He showed us, and indeed it was to many a revelation, what a splendid medium for literature the speech of the common people was . . . in the hands of an expert.

Coming as he did from this *muintir*-centred culture, O'Leary's autobiography contains much flesh-and-blood social history. 'My own Story' he called it, but it is also the story of his people. He cannot even begin with himself, but naturally goes back three centuries to the battle of Kinsale, to the downfall of the Gaelic order which had prevailed for a millennium and a half. He next moves on to 1642 when his castle-owning ancestor, Cnogher Merygagh O'Leary (as the English state papers called him) was attainted by Lord Cork at Youghal. Aristocrats in 1642, tenant farmers with the grass of seven cows 200 years later—that was the history of his branch of the family and, except for the fact that they were better off than most of their *muintir*, it was a history of Ireland in miniature.

His race-memory of traditional rebellion and resistance differed in emphasis from most modern histories. The Republic (a word he never uses) of a Wolfe Tone or a Robert Emmet can hardly be said to have been anything more than skin-deep in Irish-speaking Ireland; it was always secondary to the struggle for the land, even with regard to the rebellions of 1798 and 1867. Republicanism, in Ireland on the whole, has been English-speaking. (The Scots Gaelic world, today much stronger than the Irish, is still proudly loyal to the British monarchy and contemptuous of Scots Nationalism.) When the Canon thinks of insurrection, the ideas of the French or American Revolutions and their manifestations in Irish history are far from his mind, kept at a distance by emotional memories of the fighting dispossessed, of tories and rapparees, of Whiteboys and Ribbonmen and Captain Rock.

It must be emphasized that Canon O'Leary, the ardent nationalist, was never an advocate of physical force. He found himself on the other side of the fence to the Fenians, whom he greatly admired for the qualities which W. B. Yeats was later to immortalize by implication in poems such as *September 1913*, and while he constantly aimed at reviving the 'Romantic Ireland' which Yeats had recognized, he was equally convinced of the necessity for passive resistance and constitutional reform in Ireland's march to nationhood. Such views were swept aside by the more or less successful outcome of the 1916 Rebellion and the War of Independence, but the most recent chapter in the bloody history of the British–Irish conflict surely puts him in the right.

Nevertheless, his implacable 'hatred of English rule in Ireland' resulted in a disharmony between himself and his bishops and immediate superiors. The leaders of the Roman Catholic Church in Ireland (along with the remnants of the old Gaelic aristocracy) had, for the most part, deliberately adopted a pro-English stance, arguing that demonstrative loyalty would hasten emancipation and incalculably strengthen the position of the Church within the Union. In the event, the Church was proved right. (The Roman Catholic landholders, having first lost faith in the French monarchy's power to deliver them and then been terrified of the implications of French Republicanism, were every bit as anxious to assume allegiance to England.) Thus the Church leadership frowned, to say the least of it, upon the various nationalist and socialist movements of the period and looked askance at efforts to 'revive' the Gaelic language and culture. It could be argued that, despite the fact that not a few priests worked wholeheartedly to restore the language, the attitude of the Church was the greatest single factor in the failure of the Free State and the Republic to gaelicize Ireland, since real advances may seem to have been made in most areas of Irish life but virtually none religion-wise; to this day, the vast majority of the clergy remain, at least unconsciously, antagonistic in practice to the language.

O'Leary's uneasy relations with many of his fellow-clergy, however, had begun long before his involvement in the language revival or Land War. He was a 'scholarship boy', whose father had shown unusual independence in persuading the bishop to honour an 'arrangement' made earlier to placate some priests who were concerned that poorly off boys of good intellectual ability would be excluded from the newly-founded diocesan college. The majority of the clergy came from 'stronger' and much wealthier backgrounds; determined to leave the hardships of the Penal Days far in the past, too many had eagerly possessed themselves of their new-found status and affluence. Growing autocratic and patronizing, these considered themselves almost a new gentry; we recall that the first 'landlord' against whom Michael Davitt's Land League took action—and whom they successfully forced to reduce the rents— was the local Canon at Irishtown, Co. Mayo. (O'Leary is at great pains in the book to highlight the essential role played by so many priests in the successful struggle for the land, but does not altogether hide the frictions that existed within the Church.) While there were legitimate reasons, of course, for the clergy's suspicion of the ideas that had come from the French Revolution, the obstinate attitude of so many to what was just and necessary in the democratizing of society cannot be excused. It was to be expected that Fenianism and the Land League might be opposed as much for their inherent socialism as anything else, but education for the peasantry and working class was also too often feared and schooling considered a necessary evil.

Most bishops had welcomed the English system of National Education introduced into Ireland in 1831, although its programme was deliberately anti-national. What was worse, and arguably destructive to society with far-reaching consequences, was that the system discouraged the essentials of real education—freedom, inspiration, and imagination—while discipline was maintained with a harshness that called out for a Dickens to shame it. Even those schools set up by Roman Catholic brothers and nuns, taking their models from Victorian England, were tarred with the same brush. Despite the fact that the whole system of education in Ireland was indicted by Patrick Pearse, the future leader of the 1916 Rebellion, in his book, *Murder Machine*, published a handful of years before O'Leary's autobiography, the sorry legacy was only partly rescinded when independence came. Although Irish had already been introduced and was later made compulsory and the system, at least on the surface, had been deanglicized, freedom, inspiration, and imagination were left outside school portals—and even there stood corrected.

What O'Leary would have substituted for Gradgrind practices (he was attending his first school, at Carriganimmy, when Dickens was completing *Hard Times*) was conceived out of common sense, love, and respect for the individual, and, by no means least, the happy experience of learning from his mother at home until the age of 13. 'Here was a school then,' he writes of one he opened in Rathcormack, 'with music and reading of books. . . . We had a great time of it altogether, myself and themselves, me teaching and they learning from me and joy of mind on all of us. I don't suppose that there's another joy to be had in this life which is gladder than that joy of mind which visits a teacher and his learners when they are of one accord in their work . . .'

It was all too much for too many of his immediate superiors (the fellow was even teaching Irish!) and complaints had to be made to the bishop. His ideas on education, aligned with his other beliefs also considered incorrigible, resulted in sudden transfers and in his being passed over more than once when Parish Priests were appointed. (It must be added that his bishop did make him a full-time teacher in a diocesan Latin School and eventually gave him a parish.)

O'Leary was also 'guilty' of the cardinal sin of saying aloud that his Church was too wealthy and worldly. In his story, this criticism is all but hidden—except to the discerning reader. His account of seminary days in Maynooth concludes with some seemingly ingenuous remarks such as that schools in ancient Ireland did not have 'the grand walls around them like we had'. The description of the new church at Araglin is similarly loaded. Then he carefully records that the curate's house in Kilworth was a fine one, once the home of Baron Pigott, built on a hill a mile outside the town, and adds nothing further—we might suspect him of inconsequential rambling—until, a chapter later, he casually remarks that he took the opportunity of moving to a house in the village 'where his work was'. Nor does he forget to inform us that this latter house had previously been the doctor's. No more is said—nor is there any more to be said. '*Qui potest capere, capeat,*' he might be saying. 'If the doctor could live among the people "where his work was". . .'

An tAthair Peadar must have been well-pleased with his work in the village for he gives considerable space to it and, more significantly, uses it as a vehicle for pointing his severest moral. The edge of his criticism of the priesthood is sharpest and the cut deepest (if at first almost unsuspected, like a slit made by a scimitar), as he describes in some detail—again the undiscerning wrongly accuse him of padding—a journey from Beenamheel to Kilworth. He travels comfortably by pony-and-trap, does not feel the effects of an earth-tremor, is forced to spend the night in the cabin of a poverty-stricken woman who is to be evicted within forty-eight hours, and resumes his journey to where Baron Pigott's fine house awaits his coming. Subtly—almost too subtly, for he makes no comment—he has juxtaposed the security of the average priest with the wretchedness of so many others and shows that, as he could not feel the tremors while spanking along in his trap, so a priest living in luxury cannot feel the hardships of the poor.

Such is his method, and we lose a great deal of what is valuable in this book if we are not alert to all its implications and do not remain aware that nothing is included, no incident (no matter how trivial) mentioned, which is not used to point a moral or which does not gain significance in its context; always, the whole is greater than the sum of its parts. Undoubtedly this method of approach was dictated by his translating of the Four Gospels, on which he had been working when contemplating his story, but it is also true that the Gaelic cast of mind had always tended to be allegorical in expression.

'To the Celt', remarked Kuno Meyer, the great German scholar of Celtic, 'the half-said thing is the best.' O'Leary, whom his contemporaries often considered to be typically and even incorrigibly Irish, must be read *between* the lines. In this respect too his Irish countryman's sense of humour, sometimes droll, more often wry and chucklingly derisive, may require tuning in to. There is much more humour in this book than countless students have recognized: not for nothing did a contemporary call him 'the brightest, cheeriest, merriest of men'.

Writing his story for the converted and the imminently convertible, O'Leary assumed that his reader was familiar with much of what is now history. As he had never purposed to write a history of the events of his time nor of his own part in them, a glance at his later career may be pertinent here. He did not emerge as a national figure until his mid-50s. Whatever good work he had done for education, for the temperance movement, for the land struggle, was no more than that of the bulk of the priests engaged in these activities. He was never a politician, although he had attempted, following the Parnell 'split', to heal the self-inflicted lacerations of the nation, and later spoke out for the Sinn Féin ideal until it became too obviously a militant movement; was giving moral support to the Home Rule Party as late as 1913. It might be claimed with justification that he saw his role in life—one with and re-inforced by his priestly vocation—as an educator and propagandist, and in the Gaelic League, then an educational movement, he discovered his great opportunity.

At the age of 54 he began to write, not primarily from an irresistible creative urge, but, characteristically, to *teach*. Soon, realizing that there was 'absolutely nothing at all in the form of a book to put into the hand of a child so as to teach him Gaelic', he began a 'special book . . . with language which would suit our young people'. It was based on a folktale he had heard as a child, which, characteristically, he worked into a moral allegory. It shocked reviewers used to the Anglo-Irish novel ('There is no book to which it can be compared', wrote one of them in despair) but it took the native Gaelic world by storm. Thereafter, his was a household name.

Encouraged, he plunged into the movement to restore the language, which he saw not only as an educational force to liberate his people from the 'slave mind' bred by centuries of conquest and repression, but also as a buffer between them and the growing materialism ('paganism', he would have called it) of the western world. For the next twenty-six years of his long life he produced an average of two books a year, all, in one way or another, didactic. He wrote the first dramas in the Irish language, and another novel; he adapted—and bowdlerized—many Old and Medieval Irish tales, made translations from Latin, and even produced a version of *Don Quixote*. A great deal of his writings were religious and ranged from his translation of the New Testament to a treatise which held up the story of Job as an example for his own people. Because of the lead he gave and the paths he explored, it could be said, albeit with some hyperbole, that he created a literature single-handed.

His contribution to the living language is incalculable. Again, this was because he was primarily concerned with people. 'This little white-haired man, who became the Vice-President of the Gaelic league . . .' wrote a contemporary, J. J. Horgan, 'had a horror of red tape, taking no interest in committees, agenda or discussions but holding that the people alone could save the language and make a literature.'

With two languages at his command, he was a tireless newspaper columnist and propagandist. His personal correspondence was vast. Invariably involved in public controversy, he was a noted speaker in an age when oratory was still a force. In striving to mend the character of his people, he was helping to build a nation.

Yet, somewhat surprisingly, O'Leary saw no need in this book 'to give an account of the labours and struggles' of the Gaelic League. The fact of the matter is that he looked on his 'story' no more as a record of personal achievement than as history, but as yet another vehicle for the education of his people. He is most concerned to re-propagate (in his almost too simple, too subtle manner) the *original* spirit of the League, which at the time of writing had been taken over by the Irish Republican Brotherhood. When the Irish Volunteers were founded the previous year, Patrick Pearse had called it 'the second phase in the revolution which the Gaelic League had initiated'. The third phase, by implication, was to be the armed rebellion against British rule in Ireland. Almost without warning, the League had become political, denominational, and divisive.

It is highly possible that it was this misappropriation of a great ideal that was the initial *raison d'être* of O'Leary's 'story'. Ironically, it was in his own parish of Castlelyons that Cork's tiny part in the drama of the 1916 Rebellion was enacted. The old Canon ministered to the defeated insurgents, the Kent family, who had been among the most enthusiastic members of the branch of the Gaelic League he himself had founded there. The following year, the Gaelic League was publicly regretting his refusal to lend further support to them.

On 20 March 1920 Canon Peter O'Leary died, aged 81, still labouring undauntedly for all he had striven for for over half a century, still trusting that the pen was mightier than the sword. One of his last works was a translation of the Papal Encyclical on social justice, *Rerum Novarum*. Almost coincident with his death, which occurred on the same day that the Crown police murdered the Lord Mayor of Cork, came the publication of yet another translation, significantly and appropriately, the Book of Maccabees. He was struggling to add the finishing touches to his life of Christ when he died. More books were published posthumously.

For a time, at least, it seemed that what he had once remarked had indeed come true: 'I will be alive after my death.' Today he is almost forgotten, almost considered irrelevant. What is worse, even the well-meaning often misinterpret his mission—a plaque to his memory was recently placed on (of all places!) Baron Pigott's house in Kilworth. Recalling that Irish history is replete with miracles of revival and restoration, I like to hope that (to paraphrase his esteemed Shakespeare), the good An tAthair Peadar did is not interred with his bones.

CYRIL Ó CÉIRÍN
Luimneach, 1987

NOTE: Not all the original material is included in this translation and the order has been slightly altered. Unfortunately, the major—and culpable— omission, in my 1969 edition, of Chapters 10, 11, and 13 cannot now be redressed. These pages, almost entirely given over to boyhood hikes in the mountains of West Cork and Kerry, deal allegorically with the attractions and temptations natural to adolescence. Some few pages each from chapters 19 and 28 of the original have not been included, much smaller amounts from chapters 14, 15, 16, 17, 18 and 19.

CHAPTER I

MY ANCESTORS

IN the year of Our Lord 1602, beside Kinsale, the Gaeil and the two Hughs, Hugh O'Neill and Hugh Roe O'Donnell, were broken in battle[1]. At that time, the people of Ireland had been violently fighting against the enemy for the cause of Éire and for the cause of the faith during the nine years previous, and in that time they had been victorious over the Foreigners in every serious battle fought between them until that defeat of Kinsale. That single defeat ruined the victorious march of nine years and Ireland was once again under the heels of the enemy.

Then came the iron heel and the havoc, the foul deed in the shape of law and the falsehood in the shape of truth. The Gaeil were driven from the lands of their fathers, when they would not deny their faith, and the land was given to foreign robbers over from England and Scotland – until the very vehemence of the injustice forced the Gaeil to rise again and to make another attempt to protect themselves from such a destruction.

Forty years after the Kinsale disaster it was, when they rose again. When this insurrection of 1641 was threatening, a certain poet said:

In the year forty, no bloom on the furze will grow,
And the very year after, the English will all be laid low.

The saying so nearly came true! Owen Roe O'Neill, brother's son to Hugh O'Neill, came over to Ireland and was placed in command of the Gaeil of Ulster. As was hereditary to him, he was a prudent, courageous and able man, trained in war and in the business of war. A great many sons of the nobility, who had been banished after the defeat of Kinsale, came over from Spain and from France and from other places in Europe, so that it wasn't long until there were strong hostings of the Gaeil in each of the provinces of Ireland and they were standing up for their rights.

They persevered until Owen Roe O'Neill, at the battle of Benburb, did exactly the same deed as his father's brother and Red Hugh O'Donnell did at the battle of the Yellow Ford ten and forty years before.

The nobility, both Gaelic and Old Foreigners[2], were gathered in Kilkenny at that time, making laws and regulations for the people of Ireland; the English were powerless to interfere or to prohibit the business. But when Owen Roe O'Neill won that terrible victory at Benburb, some of the other Gaelic nobles became jealous. By degrees, the hate grew and spread, as did the bad blood they had towards him and between themselves. On top of that, there came disunity between the Gaeil and the Old Foreigners in the Council of Kilkenny. The enemy made every endeavour, by conspiracy, calumny and guile, to incite each side against the other – granting half-favours in circumstances that one side would accept and the other would not – until the hate, which the nobles of the Council and the chiefs of the armies had for each other, was greater than either of them had for the enemy. After nine years, the Kilkenny affair had fallen to pieces so utterly that it was as if there had been another defeat like that of Kinsale. Then came Cromwell. He brought destruction and havoc to bear on the Gaeil and their faith, a destruction to which that following Kinsale was as nothing.

After the Kinsale defeat, although the Foreigners had won the victory, their hearts were full of fear of the Gaeil. Because of this, they made peace with them. It was not a real peace, however, but one for the purpose of treachery and intrigue. Not long after it was made, the treachery began. The Foreigners pretended that they had knowledge of the planning of another insurrection against the king of England. To plan so was a deadly crime – if it could be confirmed. To confirm it, nothing was required other than to seize, one by one, the Gaelic nobles and bring them for trial over to London, where, if they were found guilty, they were given to the gallows. The Gaelic nobles were well-aware of the knavery; by this time, they had bought well-founded sense. They knew they had done no crime, had planned no insurrection, nor had any idea of the kind; they wanted nothing but leave to be at peace and rest after nine years' war. Yet they knew, besides, that when the law of England went into action against a person, that neither honesty nor innocence was any defence for him, especially so if he had land, or lordship, or wealth to lose.

The Gaelic nobility were well aware of these matters at the time, and they fled from Ireland before the foreign knavery – trying. sentencing and hanging – could be played on them.

When they were gone, the king and the Foreigners were satisfied. They thought nothing better than that the nobles of the Gaeil should flee for their lives. Left behind them was the grand, long, extensive land of the Province of Ulster – exactly the same as it would have been left behind them if they had stayed to be hanged.

The enemy wanted nothing else. They took the land and divided it between them.

It was the nobles of highest degree who went from the Province of Ulster that time. The great nobles of Munster had gone before that. That left in Ireland, north or south, only the smaller gentry and the poor. Ten and forty years after that, when the destruction of Cromwell was complete, a murderous effort was made to clear the entire Gaelic race, both nobles and commons, from the land, by expulsion or death. They would not accept the new faith, no matter what persuasion or force was used to that end – neither through inclination nor force would they accept it. For that reason, the enemy reckoned that nothing could be done with them but to exterminate them completely. They had their own motives for doing so: when the great nobles would be expelled from Ulster, the land of Ulster would go to themselves. If it had been possible to kill or expel from Ireland the entire race of the Gael, all the land would have been left for the enemy. And, behind the pretext of religion, it was the land they wanted.

Although the devastation that followed the defeat of Kinsale, weighed heavily on the great Gaelic nobles, the smaller gentry escaped it. But Cromwell's devastation came on all classes of the Gaelic race, both nobles and commons. It spread throughout the land, into lonely glens and out-of-the-way places, so that no area or class escaped it. Those, who at that time were dwelling in those out of the way places (and whose ancestors before them had been there for hundreds of years and for scores of generations), dwelling pleasantly and quietly, free from the affliction and distress of the wars which were continuously going on about them – these, also, were overtaken by Cromwell's devastation. They were plundered and destroyed. Those, who were not put to death, were forced to fly for their lives from these ancient dwelling-places, and set off for the corners of the earth, as poor as they were alive.

At that time, in the west of Iveleary in Munster, there was a castle, which was not over-great, called the Castle of Carrignacora. Two brothers were dwelling there; Diarmuid O'Leary and Conor O'Leary were their names. The devastation overtook them. They were forced to go away and leave both castle and territory to some foreign stranger[3]. They came from the south to Ballyvourney. One of them married a woman of the Dineens who was living on Ullanes, and he stayed there. According to what I was told, that was Conor. Diarmuid went over to a place which used to be called Carrignamadry, and he settled there. Some time afterwards, one of

Conor's family went north to Duhallow and he went to live on the Mullaroe, four miles to the north of Millstreet, beside Cullen. He married a woman called Eveleen of Rylane; I think she was an O'Callaghan. They had a son—Conor was his name—a very wise, very prudent man. He married one of the Hickeys, a daughter of Tadhg 'ach Aindriais, who was living over at Dromathane, on the banks of the Blackwater; the daughter was called Neill ní Taidhg.[4] They had the full of the house of children. Siobhán was the name of one of the daughters.

Diarmuid, according to what I was told, was living on Carrignamadry. He had a son, Conor. When this Conor was married and doing for himself, he had a servant who was also called Conor and was of the O'Leary people as well, so, as a result, the pair were known as 'Conor the master' and 'Conor the boy'. Conor the master had off-spring, but they died as quickly as they came. Himself and his wife were very distressed over this. It came about, once, that they were expecting yet another member of the family. The time was approaching, but, if it was, they were both distressed and afraid that the child would go from them as all the others had done before that—so much so that, if there had been no other matter to cause the damage, the mother's affliction of mind alone would be great enough to do so. Some days before the time came for the child's arrival, a woman, whom nobody had ever seen before, came in the door to them. The man of the house asked her where she was from.

'I came a long way from home to ye here,' she said, 'from Kildare to the north.'

Then she looked at the wife.

'Let there be no distress nor fear on you this time,' she said. 'The one who is now coming, will live—but only on one condition,' she said. 'Let him be given a name other than a family one, and he will live.'

When she had said that much, she went from them out the door and nobody ever saw her alive or dead, in the place after that.

It wasn't long until the child came—a little son. Conor or Diarmuid or Art or Céadach or Fear, these were the names which went with his family; but this son was called Barnaby, a name that was never heard before on any of the O'Leary people. Another son came after him. They continued turning their backs on the family tradition and he was given Peter as a name. The two of them lived and turned out to be fine, big men. Barnaby married and had two sons; one he called Jeremiah (Diarmuid), in spite of the turning from tradition, but the second son he called Peter, his brother's name.[5]

When the sons were grown ups Barnaby had to leave Carrignamadry; I was never able to find out what the reason was.[6]

At the same time as that, there was a man by the name of Daniel Toohey living northwards in Glendav, at the foot of Mullaghanish. He had two daughters, Siobhán and Maura Toohey. On the southern side of Glendav, there is a townland with the name of Liscarrigane, which was up for letting[7] at the time Barnaby O'Leary and his two sons were leaving Carrignamadry. Daniel Toohey took this land on let and, when he had made two farms of it, he gave them to his two daughters, to Siobhán and Maura. He had a very great opinion of the two sons of Barnaby O'Leary. He made the two matches with them. He gave Siobhán to Jeremiah and Maura to Peter and settled them onto the two farms on Liscarrigane. There was the grass of one and twenty cows in each farm and the two couples were young and strong, fit to take from the land whatever good it possessed. But it was not good land, being wild and wet, for the most part. Still, two big, strong families of high character were reared on it. Each couple had a houseful of children. Peter O'Leary and Maura Toohey had fifteen or sixteen of a family; Jeremiah was the name of their eldest boy.

When the time came around for it, a match was mentioned between this Jeremiah and Siobhán O'Leary, the daughter of the Conor O'Leary who was at that time living northwards on the Mullaroe, beside Cullen. It was recognized as being the makings of a good match. It was recognized, also, that there was a blood relationship there and that it might be necessary, perhaps, to obtain a dispensation on its account. The relationship was counted,[8] on the two sides, right back to the two brothers, Diarmuid and Conor O'Leary, that pair who were banished from the Castle of Carrignacora; from the reckoning it was found that the relationship was farther out than the fifth degree. The match was made. Jeremiah Roe O'Leary, son of Peter O'Leary and Maura Toohey, of Liscarrigane, was married to Siobhán O'Leary, daughter of Conor O'Leary and Nell Hickey, from the Mullaroe. In the year of the age of Our Lord, a thousand eight hundred and thirty-nine, the pair had a son. I am that son.[9]

NOTES TO CHAPTER I

1. I have been persuaded to use for the most part the common anglicizations of personal and place names. However, as the Gaelic forms contain a wealth of meaning for the Irish-speaker which the anglicized forms can never be expected to possess, I have supplied in Appendices 1 and 2 the Irish forms—and their meanings—of such names which occur in those parts of the book where Irish was the language in question or where the traditional associations were important. I have also included information which may assist in indicating the associations the names would have had for a native-speaker such as Canon O'Leary.

2. A term used to describe the Roman Catholic descendants of the pre-Tudor colonists since the coming of the Normans.

3. This meant far more than a mere interchange of lords, as the use of the two words, 'foreign' and 'stranger' suggest. See Appendix 6.

4. Up to recent times wherever Irish was spoken, a person's recent genealogy was included in his full name—a necessary distinction owing to the predominance of certain surnames in any given district and also to the fact that each family group made use of the same traditional Christian names. Neill ni Taidhg 'ach Aindriais Uí hIcídhe, therefore, might be anglicized to Nell, daughter of Tadhg, (who was) a son of Andrew Hickey.

In the project-bibliography given at the end of this book, I note under 'Folkways' a magnificent body of folklore collected some 40 years ago, *Leabhar Sheáin Í Chonaill* ('John O'Connell's Book). In a simple but impressive opening, the Kerry farmer and fisherman goes to great pains in introducing himself—in bald translation, something like this: 'The O'Connell people are here for the length of time that I am the fifth or sixth generation of them. I am Maurice's Daniel's John, (Maurice was) son of Séartha, a son of Séartha, descendant of Conall. We are known as 'the Séarthas', because there used to be a Séartha in every generation of them until recently.' This man could name all the family members of at least three generations in his family tree!

5. An important point about this tale is that Canon O'Leary accepted it without question and it seems to have influenced his later devotion to St Brigid of Kildare. Almost certainly the tale was 'invented' to explain away to the children something the elders of the family considered shameful—the adoption of English names in the place of traditional Gaelic ones. Such foreign names were called *cúl-le-cine*, 'anti-racial', with the metaphoric sense of turning one's back on one's heritage. It is likely that Barnaby O'Leary was born after the defeat of Bonny Prince Charlie had ended the hopes of Jacobite Ireland. From this on, the upper- and middle-class Catholics would take every opportunity to protest their loyalty to the crown—the well-documented history of Daniel O'Connell's family affords a perfect example. Christian names changed radically from this on. Sometimes, as in the case of Canon O'Leary's great-grandfather, there was a complete break with tradition but usually an attempt was made to find an English name which approximated in sound to the 'race name', e.g. Jeremiah for Diarmuid, Thaddeus for Tadhg, Daniel for Dónal, Arthur for Art,

Cornelius for Conchubhar, etc. (In this translation, I have, for the most part, followed this custom.)

6. The chapter 'The Big House' in Corkery's *The Hidden Ireland* is worth reading, treating as it does of the O'Leary house in the Carrignamadry area.

7. From 1750, minor concessions were being given to the Roman Catholics. The Bogland Act was passed in 1771, enabling them to take leases of not more than 50 acres of bad land for 61 years.

8. The knowledge of one's genealogy (the ability to 'trace' as it is known today) had a very practical function, therefore, in marriage settlements and in heirships. The later intermarriage in many areas might not have occurred to the same degree had not the knowledge of blood-ties died out with the Irish language. Such knowledge was, of course, a factor in laying claim to lands and, up to a century ago, peasants in mud-cabins still hoped to regain estates confiscated from their ancestors.

9. See Appendix VII, Canon O'Leary's Ancestors.

CHAPTER II

IN LISCARRIGANE

My grandfather and grandmother, Peter O'Leary and Maura Toohey,[1] had eight sons and eight daughters. They had two fine farms of land, one with the grass of one and twenty cows at Liscarrigane and the other, with the grass of fifteen head, down at Kilgobnet. It was good enough, but it wasn't too great a property from which sixteen children could be raised and settled in life. If the father had lived until he'd have been up to seventy or so, perhaps he might have something of real benefit for his family, but—God bless the hearers!—death came for him when he was but eight and forty. Although the time he had for it was short, before he died he had arranged marriages for most of the daughters and these were well settled. However, there was nothing he could do for the sons but to divide the land between them. He willed Liscarrigane to four of them, half to one pair and half to the other. One of this four died soon after his father. The three who were left then made three thirds of the farm between them, so that each of them only had the grass of seven cows. One of those three brothers was my father.[2]

A person might say that no man would show good sense in taking a young woman to him and settling himself to live on a small farm of that sort—the grass of seven cows and nothing in it but bad land. Undoubtedly it would not show good sense if he had any other opportunity of making a different bargain for himself: but he had not. None of the people of Ireland had any other prospect at that time but the land. Then, and for hundreds of years before then, both they and their ancestors had been cut away from any kind of livelihood but that of working the land so as to make revenue for the landowners—and they would have been cut away from this as well had there been any other way of getting an equal amount of revenue. Besides, when my father and mother were first married, things were in no way as bad with the farmers as they were to become a little while later. Potatoes were growing well and good money was to be had from butter. The butter made the rent and so every other produce which could be taken from the ground was the farmer's own. The potatoes and milk maintained the household, while the strip of linen and the wool of three head of sheep was enough to clothe them.

It is true that at the time people had a poor opinion of the potatoes and the sup of milk as food.[3] But now, when I look back at those days, at the food and the people who were reared on it, I have this much to say: the men and women were much more energetic and healthy than they are here today. At that time, you would never see a boy or girl without the full of their mouths of fine, strong, bright teeth—and with every tooth as hard and fast as a small rock. What do you see nowadays? No sooner do the teeth grow in the children's mouths than they are rotting and decaying and turning into nothing but stumps—and the child has to get false teeth in or he wouldn't be able to take food at all! What brings the rot and decay in their teeth? Bad stomachs. And what causes the bad stomachs? What else would but unwholesome food. Everyone knows that unwholesome food which plays havoc with the teeth must be doing great damage to the entire body. And we all know that no *garsún* or little *cailín* can be in their right health if the teeth are wasting away in their mouths like that. If people would only throw away the tea and the white loaf and start taking potatoes and milk as their food and drink again, or eating wheaten bread instead of that white loaf, they'd have teeth and stomachs and health every bit as good as their fathers had.

I think that the memory that is farthest back in my head is that of being in the arms of some woman, I don't recall now who she was. She was standing facing out the door so that I had a view out over the townland which used to be called Caharinduff and of the hill known as Derryleigh. There was—and still is!—a long, toothed, gapped ridge on that hill, and I well remember getting a surprise from seeing the teeth and the gaps which were between and asking myself what was the cause of the hill to be so roughly shapen. I recall how I later got to know the hill on the northern side of Derryleigh; it was called the Curraleigh.[4] I recall that later still I used to see, from our door to the south-east, a house with trees around it. Somebody told me that it was Siobhan Buckley's house at Bawnatanaknock. Siobhan Buckley[5] had a son, Conor Corkery was his name. I got to know him when we were both grown up. A decent, respectable man he was and a good neighbour.

After some time, I was able to set off into the yard and to go east to the corner of the haggard from where I had a view, not only across to Caharinduff and the Derryleigh and north-eastwards to the Curraleigh, but also over all the rest of our land. It was not good land. The greater part of it was wild and had never been tilled. There was a road from the corner of the haggard across to a place we used to call the Moorland's Edge, where a little road crossed it. There was a house at the cross and the old woman who lived there was known as Peg of the Cross. A nice, affectionate woman she was. She hadn't one word of English, but she spoke a very fine, very flavoured Gaelic. The blessing of God on her soul![6]

The corner of the moorland on the other side of the road from the house of Peg of the Cross was known as Moorland Corner. That moor belonged to us, and there was no profit in it. Nothing but heather grew on it—and not much of that itself. The field in Moorland Corner was broken into afterwards and we called the little field we had made there the Little Field of Moorland Corner.

A little while to the north-east of the Little Field of Moorland Corner and from Peg of the Cross's house, there was another small house, where lived a son of Peg's. He was married to a woman of the Creedons. This woman was called Maire Ruadh and Peg's son was Larry. The couple had a daughter, Peg, known as Larry's Peg.[7] She had not one word of English, nor had her father. This was the little girl who used to be telling the stories to us. It was she told that story, 'Séadna'. When we were all pretty young, I listened to her tell it; I kept it in my head and put it down in a book many years after.[8] I don't suppose there is any sign of Peg's house to be seen at the cross now, nor the pick of a sign of the other house either. I don't know where Larry's Peg is now or if she lives at all. Larry himself and Maire Ruadh have been dead for a great length, may it turn out to be for the good of their souls!

I heard of a thing Maire Ruadh did when the bad times were here and, perhaps, it'd be no harm to tell of it now. At that time, it was the potato garden kept every poor person in existence, that is, with whatever sup of milk he would get from the farmer who had a place for him as a workman. The farmer used to give a half-acre of manured land to the workman and he in turn would pay through his work for his little house and the half-acre. They'd have a tally-stick and each would keep the account on it. It's how the tally-stick was split into two halves, the workman keeping one and the farmer the other. When the account was to be put down, they would come together, each with his own part of the stick. Then, for example, if the workman had done five days' work, the pair would lay the two half-sticks side by side and either one of them would cut five notches with a knife across the two half-sticks, a notch or a mark for every day's work done. The marks were cut in such a way that the knife would lie on the two sticks at once and so that each mark would be cut into both of them. Then, each man would retain his half of the tally-stick and neither would be able to do an injustice to the other, because a notch could not be cut or put in without the two half-sticks being laid together again; when this would be done, the marks would have to come together exactly, just as when they were first cut.

Before the blight came on the potatoes, there used to be such a good crop that any household, which was not too big, would have a good sufficiency of food for the year from the amount of potatoes in the half-acre of manured land. If there was a big household, they would just have to have extra land in their garden. They knew no other kind of food and, if they did itself, they simply had no means of getting it. That left them in a terrible plight whenever the blight used to come on the potatoes.[9]

But about Maire Ruadh. She and Larry had a garden. The blight came on it. I heard her telling how she had spent the day, when the stalks were rotting and falling, looking at the garden and she crying, and she not knowing in the world where they would get anything to eat. The garden was no good now. When they'd eaten whatever food was in the house, the hunger greatly affected poor Larry. He got the rheumatics and wasn't able to rise from the bed. Maire had to go out 'gathering' (as they used to call it), seeking for alms. That woman used to out in the morning and she on a black-fast; and she'd go west to Clydagh, over the hills, four or five miles of a journey. She had some relations there. A small can of milk used to be given to her there and she'd bring that away home with her. She'd put it on the fire until it was curds and whey. Then, she'd give the curds to Larry and she herself used drink the whey. The woman kept up this practice until poor Larry died. I don't know where there was another 'lady' who would have done it at the time. The strong faith that was inside in her heart, it was this which obliged her to do the deed.

But there was nobody in Ireland thinking of black potatoes the first day that I stood at the corner of the haggard, looking over to the house of Peg of the Cross, and to the Little Field of Moorland Corner, and to the house of Maire Ruadh, and to the other little fields to the west beyond that, the Field of the Mound and the Field of the Rushes; and all along to the Red Hillock and to the ravine, which had been cut down through the Red Hillock and through the bog by the stream which comes from the top of the Curraleigh. They are all there still, exactly as they were the first day I had looked across on them from the corner of the haggard. They are cold and wild and poor but, if they are itself, it is on them I prefer

to dwell in recollection when I have the leisure to do so, because on
them and on their making it was that I was thinking, when it was
first told to me that God had made the world.[10]

NOTES TO CHAPTER II

1. Peadar ua Laoghaire and Maire Ní Thuathaig. They were, of course,
Irish-speakers and, while the anglicized forms of their names were doubtless
used on official documents (such as a marriage certificate, etc.), they would
have been known locally under the Gaelic forms.
2. Canon O'Leary goes on to explain that there was nothing else his
grandfather could do, due to the social fabric of the age; such land division
led to irrevocable poverty and was, ultimately, one of the causes of the
Great Famine in the 1840s. See: C. Woodham-Smith. *The Great Hunger* (pp.
25–27). Four Square edition, 1964.   An interesting story of a slightly earlier
period is told of Denis O'Connor of Belanagare, lineal descendant of the
Connacht Kings and father of the more famous Charles O'Connor. When
one of his family showed haughty contempt for a poor man, the father
admonished him saying: 'Remember that, although I am the son of a
gentleman, you are the son of a ploughman.' The decline of the branch of
the Uí Laoghaire family on the Canon's father's side was as swift and as
disastrous. Castle-owning aristocracy in 1642, when they were attainted, his
ancestors had only two generations at the 'ploughman' stage before they
lost all their land about 1770.
3. A song of the period went:

> Prátaí ar maidin, prátaí um nóin,
> 's dá n-éireochainn í
> Meadhon oídhche,
> Prátaí a gheobhainn!

('Potatoes at morning, potatoes at noon, and if I were to rise at midnight,
potatoes I'd get!')
   But, with milk or buttermilk, the humble potato formed a scientifically
satisfactory diet. Arthur Young recognized it as being better than that of the
English labourer. See Appendix 7.
4. Litanies of placenames such as occur in these early chapters have, of
course, a much more evocative quality in the original Gaelic. In Appendix
I, the original names and their meanings are given.
5. According to Gaelic custom, a married woman retains her maiden-
name.
6. Canon O'Leary has a habit of adding a pious ejaculation for the souls of
long-departed friends who 'had not one word of English'—a juxtaposition,
which the late Myles na gCopaleen (better known internationally, perhaps,
as 'Flann O'Brien') thought so incongruous that he milked it for all it was
worth in his uproarious satire, *An Béal Bocht*. Paragraphs such as the
one which follows immediately were also obvious grist to Myles' mill.
7. In the original, 'Peig Labhráis', i.e. Peig (daughter) of Labhrás.
8. Some fifty years afterwards, in fact; *Séadna* may be said to have begun the
modern literary movement in Irish and had immense influence. It is still
probably the best-known of modern works in the language.

For a list of Canon O'Leary's works, see Appendix 5.

9. The Census of Ireland Commissioners of 1851 noted that the potato crop had failed some 24 times in the previous century and a half.

10. The reader, who is interested in the lives of the common people of the time, could do much worse than read—and enjoy—Canon O'Leary's two little books of short stories, *Ár nDóithin Araon* and *Ag Séideadh agus Ag Itheadh*. These are not short stories such as O'Connor and O'Faoláin, O'Flaherty and OConaire might have written, but the 'gearrscéalta' or droll little stories that the country folk used tell about their neighbours. 'Rud éigin ar an gCapall' is probably the most typical and the best; of it, the Canon wrote: 'I think (it) will cause a laugh. Like all my other little stories, it is a positive fact. It all took place at Liscarrigane, and I knew everyone of the persons concerned'.

CHAPTER III

ROGUES

I USED often go east to the haggard corner, but it was a long time before I went past that point. There was a little patch of unenclosed land, which was called the Old Cattlefield, to the north of the haggard. Nobody had any more right than his fellows to the Old Cattlefield, for it wasn't worth anything. There was a family of the Herlihy people living in a house behind ours. Their geese used often be in the Old Cattlefield. Among them was a great, white gander, 'a very bright, hearty fellow of a gander', and there wasn't south in Africa, nor east in the Indies, nor in any other part of the world, a wild beast which could put fear into the heart of a person like that rogue of a gander used put into my heart that time. When I would come to the haggard corner and see the geese out in the Old Cattlefield, I'd run back as hotly as another person would run from a yellow lion or from a spotted lion. If the geese were a long way from me, I'd wait a little while, perhaps, to look at them, but I'd keep my head down and stay in the shelter of a rock lest the gander would see me. At times, I would have a good view of him when he'd have none of me. My fear was no wonder. When he would lift his head and sit up straight, he was bigger by far than myself. I'd sense, at times, that the ruffian would see me well but he'd be letting on that he wouldn't. He'd have his head bent and he picking the green grass, but I'd know well that it was watching me he was and waiting to see if I would go out on the Old Cattlefield, so that he could stretch out his long, white neck and make a run at me to eat me.

Once, I went out into the Old Cattlefield when I judged that neither himself nor the geese were there at all; but they were, unbeknown to me. I noticed nothing amiss until I saw him making for me, his head to the ground and his neck stretched. I screamed and ran. I got away from him, but it was only just. He turned back and you could hear him a mile from home, boasting of the heroic deed he had done. Since then, I have often seen and heard that same screeching and boasting coming from a gander that was not a goose—from a gander of a man!—over some deed that was not one pick braver than the gander's deed on the Old Cattlefield yon time.

There's a field in front of the door and we used call it 'the field outside'. There was a gap, for going into the field, just opposite the door. When the gander'd be in the Old Cattlefield, I'd sometimes strike out east through the gap and down the middle of the field. From there, I'd have a view north to Knockboy, and to the Keel, where another gander altogether was killed after that, and to Glendav, where Tadhg of the Eggs was living; and up to the Rock of the View and to Casserly's Tower, and down to the Field of the Stones and the Field of the Bog-cutting, and to the Field of the River and the Field of the Sand. I got to know them all, one after the other. Small, poor, hard fields they were. The whole place was bad land. Yet before the blight came on them, the potatoes would grow well in any kind of land—and fine, sound, abundant food they made, for people or cattle or horses or for any living thing that could eat food at all. Now and again, perhaps, there would be a year when the gardens would fail, through drought or through some ill-wind or because of a disease having been in the seed, in such a way as would leave the potatoes too tiny or would make nothing beyond the stalks. That would give a year of scarcity to the people; a lot of them would have 'Big Conor in the corner'. There would not be much other kinds of food in the country. Whatever grain of corn was cultivated, it (or most of it) would have to be sold to make up the rent. People would do their best to keep enough of the little potatoes as would sow the garden for the coming year. Then, perhaps, the weather would be fruitful in the coming year and the gardens would grow luxuriantly, so luxuriantly that the potato-beds would be hidden under a heavy carpet of white flowers at Summer's end and new potatoes to be had on Lammas Eve—the full of a potato basket under every stalk, of food that beat anything a person ever put in his mouth. For the rest of that year, nobody would think back on 'July of the cabbage'.

The reason that month was called 'July of the cabbage' is this: when the bad years would come, there would be nothing during that month for the people to eat but cabbage. Then, when Lammas Eve would come and the new potatoes, there would be great joy on everybody because 'July of the cabbage' was at an end.

When I'd have paid my visit to the field opposite the door, I'd go east to the field beside it. The Humpy Field we called it, for it was high in the centre as if it had a hunch. I think it was from the height in the humpy field that I got my first sight of the yellow field and of the little lump of a field below it, which was called 'Patrick's Height'. Why it was called 'Patrick's Height' I don't know, unless it was that someone reckoned that it had some resemblance to the Ardpatrick north of the Redchair in County Limerick. Whatever in the world was the reason, I knew the Patrick's Height in our land long before I came across the other.

I think that it was also when standing in the middle of the Humpy Field, on top of the hunch, that I laid my eyes for the first time ever on Daingean na Saileach, the Fortress of Sally Trees. I saw it to the south-west and didn't it look rough hewn, forbidding and rugged. You might well call it a fortress. A person would think that no living thing would be able to enter it—and that if anything did go in among those rocks, that it would have no chance of ever getting out again, they were so massive and so overwhelming. But why was it called the Fortress of Sally Trees? There wasn't as much as the tiniest twig of a sally rod or of an ashplant or anything else to be seen on its jagged rocks, from north to south or top to bottom. However, that's the way it was the first day I saw it from the middle of the Humpy Field and I was told after that the rocks were not always so exposed. A man, who was three score years of age when I was born, said to me that the Fortress of Sally Trees was thickly covered with woods when he himself was a boy, and that there was nothing to prevent a person going on the branches of the trees from the northern end to the southern, without putting a foot to the ground. The timber was knocked, but the name of the little hill remained.

When there was corn in the field opposite the door, I would not be able to go into it and go east, for the corn used to be a good deal higher than myself and I'd go astray in it. Then, when the corn would be reaped, I wouldn't be able to go east through the field because there were little stems and prickly stumps in the stubble field that would prick my feet. No children, or young people, had shoes that time. People, who were grown up itself, wouldn't have shoes or stockings except on Sundays, when they'd be going to Mass, or on a day they'd be going away somewhere. Signs on it, they used have hard, healthy feet and didn't give a jot for the cold. Now, shoes must be put on a child long before he's able to walk or to put a foot on the ground at all. That leaves a lot of them with weak feet—a weakness which stays all their lives. The old way was better.

I recall a certain day when I was, I suppose, three years of age. There was corn or stubble in the field opposite the house, so that I was forced to stay inside. I was riding a stick that I had, up and down the floor, pretending it was a horse. I saw a lot of strange people, whispering and talking, out in the yard. I realized that some important person was coming and that they were waiting for him. I'd hear every now and again the word 'the master' and 'Mr Saunders'. At last, a big, well-fed gentleman came in. He sat in a chair in the centre of the house and the strangers all crowded in after him. My father was one of the crowd which came in. It was he had put the chair in the centre for the gentleman to sit on. There wasn't a word out of anybody. I had no backwardness nor fear of any person, high or low, at that time (unless it was of the gander!) so over with me and I stood facing the gentleman.

'Good morrow, Mr Saunders!' I said to him, welcoming him in English.

'Oh, good morrow, boy! good morrow, boy!' he said, and he took me by the shoulder and drew me to him until I was between his two knees.

'Tell me, my boy,' he said, 'did you eat any meat today?'

'Don't you know,' I said, on the spot, 'that I ate a piece of a goose long ago when it was Christmas!'

I thought the hot, dry soul would fall out of everyone, who was present, with the dint of laughter. The gentleman himself also laughed and turned me loose.

I recall that as well and as sharply as if it had occurred yesterday or a week ago. I recall, also, the surprise I got when I saw them all putting their souls out laughing at the thing I'd said; but a day came, a little while afterwards, when I understood right well what had set them laughing.

The 'master' had come to raise the rent on them all. When he put the question about the meat to me, it is how he was looking for an excuse. If I had said that I had eaten meat that morning, or the day before, or a week before, he would have the excuse he required. He would be able to say: 'Ye have meat to eat every single week. This indicates that ye have my land too cheaply. Ye must give me more rent.' But when the child could only boast that he had eaten a bit of a goose 'a long time ago when it was Christmas', the feet were knocked clean from under any excuse he might have had for raising the rent. That's what put them all laughing. The gentleman himself laughed, but I think the laugh he made was 'the laugh of burnt Seán'. He turned me loose fast enough at any rate; he didn't want any more of the goose.

I don't think he could have raised the rent that time, anyway. The tenants had a lease on the land. It wasn't all that easy to raise the rent on them until the lease would fall due.[1] All the same, however, the type of lease was an unfortunate one: a lease held in partnership. This gave a great advantage to the master. If one of the tenants left the rent unpaid, the master could compel the others to pay it in his place.

In the year of Our Lord, a thousand eight hundred and one, the lease had been made. At that time exactly, the 'Bonaparte times' were beginning. Before long, there was big money to be had for every single thing the farmer had to sell. The master realized that and his heart was broken because the lease prevented him from raising the rent. Himself and his agent set about every sort of intrigue to see if they could break the lease. This was the plan they settled on towards that purpose. Among the tenants, there was a man whose rent was never ready when it used to be in demand. It was let go for a few years until he was a lot in arrears. Then, the rent that he owed was demanded from the others. A great legal wrangle arose out of that. It was no small thing, when everyone had to pay his own rent already. The master reckoned that he could break the lease. After much expense and much legal wrangling, they paid up, but the law gave them the man's land until such time as they would get their own share back out of it. Some while afterwards, the same sort of wrangling again arose.

I can't recall if there was ever a day without a dispute of that kind until the lease ended, about the year 1874. Then the rent was raised to the firmament—but hardly a bit of this high rent was paid. Most of it remained unpaid until the strike, which was put up against rack-rents, came about. As a result and under the new laws, the land is now bought out by the families of the people who had spent all that earlier time fighting against injustice.

NOTE TO CHAPTER III

1. Leases, in fact, were by no means common. Sometimes it was the landlord who was at fault, as he wished to have his tenants more completely under his thumb; sometimes it was at the tenant's own wish, as he would have had to pay some £10 stamp-duty which, in many cases, he simply did not possess. Then, there was the 'hanging gale' practice, by which a new tenant might be allowed to get into arrears and so lose any protection his lease might otherwise have afforded him.

CHAPTER IV

A LEGAL WRANGLE

I RECALL, and I very young, being seated in the corner beside the fire on a winter's evening. Old Jeremiah O'Leary, father's brother to my father, was seated on a chair out from me on the same side of the fire—signs on it, his hound, which came with him, was lying between the legs of the chair. Himself and his hound used often come like that to us, when the long nights would be in it, and he'd give over a while in the beginning of the night to talking and telling old stories. The night I'm speaking of, it happened that he was discoursing on the first legal wrangle to arise among the tenants because of the lease being held in partnership among them. This wrangle arose long before I came into the world. My father was only a child at the time. One of the tenants was living on the northern side of the hill, at the foot of the Ravens' Cliff. That side of the hill was called Dermot and Grania's Bed and the southern side, where we lived, Liscarrigane.

The lease was some years in existence. The grand, big money was to be had for every single thing, because of Bonaparte's wars. The 'master' was annoyed and vexed because he had no power to raise the rent. It's how he and the steward decided to give the tenant on Dermot's Bed his head and not to demand one halfpenny of the rent for a long time. They let on that it was through pity for him that they did it. They let on that they didn't like to be hard on him; he usen't have the rent when it was in demand and the others were paying. When he was out such an amount that they thought the others would refuse to pay it in his stead, they put the law into motion. The others defended the case. After a lot of trouble and expense, they defeated the master. They paid the rent in place of the man who had held back but, until they would get their own share back out of it, the use of his farm was given to them. Then it was that all the mischief started up. The man with the farm would give them neither land nor money. They had to go through another legal proceedings to put him out of possession, but, when they had legal authority for possession, they themselves had to go and put him out, or take him prisoner, without any assistance from the king's soldiers.

A company of them gathered. Some of them were swift, strong

and young. There was a man among them who had a great left-handed cast—anything he would throw a stone at with the *ciotóg,* he would hit. Daniel Toohey was his name. They had no firearms. They set off for the house.

Before they got too close to the house, the man they wanted came out and he had a gun. When they saw the gun, some of them halted. Dan Toohey readied two stones, a stone in each of his hands and walked coolly towards the man with the gun. He lifted the gun and levelled it towards Dan. Daniel did not flinch. He walked step by step towards the gun. Dan wished to get inside the range of his own shot from the gunman. When the gunman found him coming too close to him, he took accurate aim at him and pulled the trigger. The hammer struck its blow, but fire failed. Dan kept on coming. The other man raised the gun again and made another effort to shoot the bullet. Fire failed the second time. Fire failed the third time. At last, Dan was as close as he wished to be. He threw the left-handed missile. The gunman was struck on the forehead, just before he had an opportunity of laying his finger on the trigger the fourth time. He fell. The gun was taken from him and he was tied. When he came to, he was in a side-car and they bringing him as a prisoner to Macroom.

The only stock there was for their taking out of the place was a couple of old sheep. They were taking the Catharin road with the two sheep out before them, and the gun in the hand of one of them. They were sure that the gun was empty and that that was the reason it had failed to fire, three times one after the other. They understood that the man only wanted to frighten them; that he had no intention of killing anyone. Some quarrel arose between them. It was getting sharper. The man, who had the gun in his hand, raised it for sport, to stop the quarrel, mauryah. 'Shut your mouth or I'll shoot you!' he said to one of the pair that was making the quarrel. His finger was on the trigger. He pulled on the trigger. While pulling on it, another man struck the barrel of the gun with his hand and turned it aside. The bullet went off in its full power and one of the sheep fell dead on the road.

Surprise and astonishment fell on them all. They had no other expectation but that the gun was empty. The man, who had the gun in his hand, threw himself on the caps of his two knees on the road giving thanks to God that it wasn't a person he had killed in the place of the old sheep. And the person whom he might have killed was the same Daniel Toohey, who was after laying the prisoner low a little while before with the stone he threw from the *ciotóg.*

'*Airiú*, ye hangman,' said they all to the prisoner, 'you really intended to shoot Dan Toohey!'

The prisoner never spoke a word. They turned on him and would have rightly taken it out on him had not Dan himself been protecting him. He was taken down to Macroom and underwent whatever legal process was required. Some one of the tenants paid whatever rent was due on the farm which he was then given until he had his own share back out of it.

I was listening to that much of the story and I stuck within in the corner, and not one word of it was lost on me; and there wasn't as much as one single word of that which came my way that I had to ask what was the substance of it. I understood such talk as completely as old Jeremiah himself understood it.

CHAPTER V

TWO SWORDS OF MIND

WHEN I look back now on the type of Gaelic[1] which used to be
spoken about me at that time, and when I compare it with that
which I heard afterwards in other places, the fact impresses itself
upon my mind that it was finer, more accurate, more finished and,
in addition, more powerful as a sword of the mind than any other
Gaelic I have since come across from the mouths of men or from
books. As I compare it with other tongues, with Latin or Greek or
French (according to the way I was to learn them), it impresses my
mind as being a better mental sword than any of them. Perhaps,
Greek was better when it was alive and the Greek people speaking
it, but it is only possible for me to compare my own living Gaelic
with the Greek I found in books; as far as such a comparison goes,
my own Gaelic would be in the ascendant. It is likely that someone,
who was raised in another place or province in Ireland, might say
the same thing about the Gaelic of his home-place. But there are a
few things by which we can try the point. Before I left Liscarrigane,
I had never heard from anybody's mouth phrases such as *'Tá mé',*
'Bhí mé', 'Bhí siad'; I used always hear *'Táim', 'Bhíos', 'Bhíodar'*, etc.
Little things!—but little things that come repeatedly into conversation. A taut mode of expression, as against one that is lax, makes
for finish in speech; in the same manner, a lax mode of expression,
as against the taut, makes for speech that is deficient. Besides, the
taut speech possesses a force and a vigour that cannot be contained
in speech that is falling apart.

Outside altogether of the difference in wholeness, force and
vigour due to taut speech in place of looseness, there were other
qualities of force and vigour, of resource and clarity, in the Gaelic
about me three score and ten years ago, which I have been unable
to find in any kind of speech today, either in English or in Gaelic.
The loose mode of expression is prominent in Gaelic today and
English is nothing else, English has fallen apart completely.[2]

If it had not been for that woman who came from the north,
bringing with her the name which was not in our family tradition,
my name would not have been 'Peter'; perhaps, I would not have
lived at all. And if it were not that old Barnaby and his two sons,
Dermot and Peter, had been banished to the hills, I would not have

had Gaelic, or I would not have had it with such polish and I would
not be writing here as I am now. I am doing my best to put it down
in manuscript exactly as my ear got it from people like old
Jeremiah O'Leary, my grand-uncle, and from the likes of Michael
Dubh and Maire Ruadh and her daughter, Peg.

But if I had a good opportunity to get a fine knowledge of Gaelic
from the first moment that speech began to come to me, I had a
good opportunity, also, to get English equally well, and from the
same moment. Here is how it happened. As I have said, my
mother's father, Conor O'Leary, was living on Mullaroe, four
miles north of Mill Street. He had a big farm of land there—and
good land it was, not like the bogs and rocks of Liscarrigane. He
had the grass of forty cows from that land and he was fairly wealthy
and independent. In addition to his being wealthy, he was a man of
high character, esteemed by his neighbours, high and low. A very
respectable woman among high and low, also, was the woman he
had married, Nell Hickey, i.e. Neill ní Taidhg, daughter to Tadhg
'ach Aindriais, who was over at Dromathane, like I said. They had
five sons and three daughters. The family got a good education—that is, according to opportunity at the time of giving any
form of an education to families in Ireland. Two of the daughters,
as soon as they were of an age for it, were sent to Killarney to school
and two of the boys were sent to a Latin school. One of these two
went into the college afterwards to be a priest, but, when he had
spent some years there, he realized that he had not received the call
from God to be a priest. He came home and set about teaching a
Latin School in Kanturk. A while before he left the college, his
father had died. The two daughters had then come home from
Killarney. One of them, Nell, was married to a man called Richard
O'Leary, who was living west of Knockanerribul, five miles north-
east of Killarney, and the other daughter went east to Kanturk to
her brother, for the purpose of giving him assistance in the school.
Along with other things taught to her in Killarney was some
French; it isn't likely that the French was taught to her in a way that
a man from France could have understood her, but they taught her
as well as they were able.[3] When she went to her brother to assist
him in the school, it was English and French she used to be
teaching; he taught Latin and Greek. Then, when she was twenty-
four years or so, herself and my father were married and she came
to Liscarrigane.

She took with her many books,—English and French books. As
soon as I was able to take in any teaching, she began teaching

English to me, and then she began teaching French to me, so that I was often deaf from people, who would come in or who would meet up with me outside, asking me to speak French to them!

Whatever kind the French was, she had competent English— better by far, and more accurate and more correct than any English taught in the schools. But it made no difference to me what kind of English was taught in the schools, because the schools were too far from me. The nearest school to us was a good five miles away—and it was well for me that I couldn't get there. If it had been closer to me, it is likely, of course, that I would have put in my days in it; and, if I had done so, the bad English would doubtless have gone to work on me. I was forced to stay at home and do whatever teaching my mother gave me, until I was matured. I was thirteen before I went into a school. I had read and re-read by this time all the English books we had at home. As soon as I had it in me to go out herding the cows, I used to have whatever book best pleased me and I reading it at the foot of a ditch or a bush or a whitethorn. The result was that I knew by heart much of Milton and of Shakespeare and of Rudeki, a book I have never seen since.

If my mother had good English and good education, she had Gaelic beautifully besides. Her father's house was only about a quarter of a mile from Cullen. There used to be grand Gaelic spoken there and throughout all of Duhallow. I myself spent some time (a year, I suppose) in Duhallow, beside Kanturk, more than ten and forty years ago. At that time, the young people of the place were growing up without having one word of Gaelic,[4] and, to make matters worse, I never heard before or since any speech as disgusting as the kind of English they had. When I would be listening to them, they would continually remind me of the proverb Jeremiah Moynihan used to say:

The people with least sense in Éire
are those without English or Gaelic.

Diarmuid lived in Cullen, and it's likely that he noticed the young people throwing their Gaelic away and speaking ugly, broken English.

At any rate, I had a great chance. I had both English and Gaelic from the cradle. If it hadn't been for the place in which I was born and reared, however, I would not have had Gaelic, and, if my mother had not given it to me, I would not have had English. And take note: if I had not both Gaelic and English as I have, I would not have had any chance at all of doing the work I have done. Whatever especial worth my English had, it would not have been of any help to me to learn Gaelic and to handle it as a sword of the mind: it is how the English would have made such handling ineffective. And whatever especial worth my Gaelic had, it would have brought the same ineffectiveness to bear on the English. But I got especial grasp of both swords of the two swords of mind, and especial knowledge of how to wield them both. Now, instead of rendering each other ineffective, it is how I have them both helping each other.

NOTES TO CHAPTER V

1. For an account of the Cork dialect of West Muskerry, see Brian Ó Cuiv. *Irish Dialects and Irish-speaking Districts*. Dublin Institute for Advanced Studies, Dublin, 1951. Part III is of especial interest.

2. The good father would be appalled at English in our own day, ruined as it has been by advertising, big business, technological jargon and journalism (See R. Graves and A. Hodge. *The Reader over your Shoulder*. Cape, London, 1947; S. Potter. *Our Language*. Penguin, Middlesex, 1961; H. Goad. *Language in History*. Penguin, Middlesex, 1958.) He would have agreed with Potter (*Language in the Modern World*, Penguin, p. 180) that 'good speech is a social convention' and that 'effective speech is the product of education and training, even in primitive and unsophisticated societies'. He would also have been in wholehearted agreement with Goad, when the latter wrote that Latin withered before the Roman Empire fell apart and not the opposite. In his youth, the Canon would not have been alone in his condemnation of slip-shod speech; in the peasant Gaelic society of his time, accurate speech and 'words at will' were marks of good breeding and personal attainment. This is the import of the poet's praise, described in Chapter 21. Indeed, as regards any verses quoted in this book, it is not so much the content that is important but the manner in which the poet expresses himself. Only the reader, who knows Irish, will, therefore, find it possible to get the full flavour of the *ex tempore* verses of Barry the Rake or of those given in Chapter 13.

3. That his mother knew French and that there were pupils learning French in the popular schools and pay-schools of those days need come as no surprise. Indeed, due to the Flight of the Wild Geese and the importance of the smuggling trade, both French and Spanish were more widely understood and spoken on the coasts of Kerry and Cork than English; the R. D. S. statistical survey of 1810 indicates that English was little known in Cork county and less in Kerry. The tradition was a long-lasting one; for example, Michael Collins's father (b. 1815) learned French from an itinerant hedge-schoolmaster, Diarmuid Ó Súilleabháin, in Sam's Cross, near Clonakilty. (See also Daniel Corkery. *Fortunes of the Irish Language*. Mercier Press, Cork, 1969.)

4. When Canon O'Leary first attended school (1852), the percentage of Irish-speakers in Cork county as a whole was 52·5%; on his death, some 70 years later, that figure had decreased to 22·2%. See Appendix 4.

CHAPTER VI

THE HUNGER[1]

As soon as understanding comes to a child, it is usual for people to be asking him what would his vocation in life be, when he would be big. I well recall that question being put to me very often. I don't recall having any other answer to give to it but the one, solitary answer: that I would be a priest. From the beginning that much was settled in my mind and I don't recall that there was ever anything other than that. Neither do I recall when my mind first settled on my becoming a priest when I would be grown up.

I know well that people used to be making fun of the story, for it was clear to everyone that my father had nowhere near the necessary capital to set about such an undertaking. As soon as I got any sense, I also knew that he hadn't got the capital, but that did not prevent me from being steadfast in my mind about becoming a priest, whatever way this would come about. If it were not for the blight coming on the potatoes and the bad times that came afterwards, I don't say that he would not have been able to give me the necessary amount of schooling. But the bad times turned everything upside down.

A strange thing—it was the big, strong farmers who were the first to fall! The man who had only a small farm, the grass of six or seven cows, kept his hold; the man with the big, broad, spacious farm was soon broken when the changed times came. He, who had only a little, lost only a little. Before this, there was no big rent or big demands on him. He was accustomed to living without much extravagance. It wasn't too difficult for him to tighten his belt a little bit more, and to answer the small demands on him without too much hardship. But he, who had a big farm, was accustomed to the expensive way of life. He was independent as long as his farm responded. When the change came, the returns from the farm came to a sudden stop. The loss, the extravagance, the demands were too great. It was impossible to meet them and they swept him off his feet. I well recall how I would hear the latest news and how it caused amazement: 'Oh! Did you hear? Such a person is burst! His land is up for sale. He's gone. He slipped away. His land is up!'

You would often hear 'His land is up!'—but you wouldn't hear at all that time 'His land has been taken by another person'. Nobody had any wish to take land. Things used to be very bad for those who had lost their land. They'd have neither food nor credit and there was nothing they could do but go looking for alms. They would not be long begging when they used to go into a decline and they'd die. As they were not accustomed to hunger or hardship, they couldn't stand it long when the hunger and hardship would come on them. Often, when the hunger was very severe, they'd have to rise and move out and head for the house of some neighbour (who, perhaps, would be as needy as themselves, or close to it) to see if they could get a mouthful of something to eat, which might take the frenzy of hunger off them.

One day, when I was eight years of age (I seem to remember that I was standing at the corner of the haggard), I saw a woman coming towards me up the hill. She was barefoot, walking very slowly and panting, as if she had been running. She was blowing so much, her mouth was wide open, so that I had a sight of her teeth. But the thing that amazed me altogether was her feet. Each foot was swollen so that, from the knee down, it was as big and as fat as a gallon-can. That sight took such a firm grip on my mind that it is before my eyes now, every bit as clear-cut as it was that day, although it is around three score years and five since I saw it. That woman had been fairly independent and free from adversity until the blackness had come upon the potatoes.

Another day—I can't tell if it was before or after that—I was inside in our house, standing on the hearthstone, when a boy came in the door. I saw the face that was on him and the terror that was in his two eyes, the terror of hunger. That face and those two eyes are before my mind now, as clear and as unclouded as the day I gave them the one and only look. Somebody gave him a lump of bread. He snatched the bread and turned his back to us and his face to the wall and he started right into eating it so ravenously that you would think he would choke himself. At the time I did not realize that I was so amazed by him or by his voracity, but that sight has stayed in my mind, and will stay as long as I live.

I remember one evening during the period, when the people were running in and out and they talking away. In the winter, it was. The night was after falling. I heard someone saying, 'It was down by Carriginanassey I heard the shout!' 'There it is again!' said another, and they all ran out. A while afterwards, they came back in with a poor, old fellow between them. They put him standing on the floor—he was hardly able to stand. I was facing him and I had a view of his features. His mouth was wide open and his lips, upper and lower both, were drawn back, so that his teeth—the amount he had of them—were exposed. I saw the two, big, long, yellow eye-teeth in his mouth, the terror in his eyes and the confusion in his face. I can see them now as well as I could see them then. He was a neighbour. It is how the hunger drove him out to see if he could find anything to eat and the poor man went astray in the bog that was below Carriginanassey. When he found himself going astray, he became afraid that he would fall into a hole and be drowned. He stopped then and began to shout. That was a custom—there was a certain shout for the purpose—for anyone going astray. Each one knew how to send up that *liúgh,* so that, when they heard it, everybody would know the meaning of it, and the people would gather and seek the person who was going astray.

There was a little stable at the head of the house. A poor person by the name of Patrick Buckley came and shelter was given to himself, his wife and two children in the stable. They stayed for some weeks there, but they had a small cabin for themselves after that. Sheila was the name of the elder of the two children. We had a serving-boy—Conor was his name—and I overheard Sheila talking to him one day.

'Con,' she said, in Gaelic.

'Coming, Sheila,' Con said.

'I have no speech now,' she said.

'*Airiú*, what else have you got, Sheila?' Con said.

'English,' says she.

'*Airiú,* what English could you have?' Con said.

'Peter's English and Seáinin-Philib's English.' (Seáinin-Philib was another poor person, who lived in a cabin beside the place.)

'But surely English is speech, Sheila?'

'English speech?' she said in amazement. 'If it was, surely people would understand it!'

One day, Sheila's mother had a handful of gravel in the little broad-bottomed pot, the griddle-oven they used to call it, as she was going to bake a cake; she was scouring and scraping the inside of the griddle-oven with the gravel.

'Oh, Mam!' Sheila said, 'is it how you'll put gravel in the cake?'

'It is,' said her mother.

Out went Sheila. She saw Con.

'Oh, Con,' says she, 'What'll we do? What'll we do at all?'

'What's on you now, Sheila?' Con said.

'The grey-green gravel my mother's putting in the cake for us and I don't know how in the world we'll be able to eat it. All our teeth'll be broken. Some of the stones in the gravel are very big. Not one of us will have a tooth left in his head. It's all right for Little Jeremiah he hasn't got any teeth at all yet.'

Little Jeremiah was Sheila's small, young brother. In with Con until he'd see what Sheila's mother was doing. When he saw what the gravel was being used for, they had a great laugh.

The famine came. Sheila and her father and mother and little Jeremiah had to go down to Macroom into the poorhouse.² No sooner were they inside than they were all separated from each other. The father was put among the men. The mother was put among the women. Sheila was put among the small girls. And Jeremiah was put among the very young children. The whole house, and all the poor people in it, was smothered in every kind of evil sickness, the people, almost as fast as they'd come in, falling down with a malady and—God bless the hearers!—dying as fast as the fever came on them. There used not be room for half of them in the house. The amount that would not be able to get in could only go and lay themselves on the bank of the river, on the lower side of the bridge. You would see them there every morning, after the night was over, stretched out in rows, some stirring, some quiet enough without any stir at all out of them. In a while, certain men would come and they would take those, who were not stirring, and they would put them into trucks. They would take them to a place beside Carrigastyra, where a great, wide, deep hole had been opened for them, and they would put them altogether down into the hole. They would do the same with all who had died in the house after the night.

It was not too long, after their going in and after his separation from his mother, that death came to little Jeremiah. The small body was thrown up on the truck and taken to the big hole, and it was thrown in along with the other bodies. But it was all the same to the child: long before his body was thrown in the hole, his soul was in the presence of God, in the joys of the heavens. It was not long until Sheila followed little Jeremiah. Her young body went into the hole, but her soul went up to where little Jeremiah was, in the presence of God, in the joy of the heavens, where she had solace and the company of the saints and angels, and the company of the Virgin Mary, and speech that was better by far than 'Peter's English and Seáinin-Philib's English'.

The father and mother were asking and questioning as often as they were able about Sheila and little Jeremiah. The children were not long dead when they heard about it. All the poor people had Gaelic. The superiors hadn't got it, or else they spoke it poorly. The poor people could often get word about each other without the superiors knowing it. As soon as the father and mother found out that the pair of children had died, such a grief and a brooding came over them that they could not stay in the place. They were separated from each other, but they found the opportunity of sending word to each other. They decided to steal away from the place. The wife's name was Kit. Patrick first slipped out of the house. He waited for Kit at the top of the Road of the Whisps. In a while, he saw her coming, but she was walking very slowly. The sickness was on her. They pushed on towards Carrigastyra. They came to the place where the big hole was. They knew that the two children were down in the hole with the hundreds of other bodies. They stood beside the hole and they wept their fill. Up on Derryleigh to the east of the Caharin was the cabin in which they had been living before they went into the poorhouse. They left the big hole and they headed north-west for Derryleigh, where the cabin was. The place was six miles of a journey from them, and the night was coming, but they pushed on. The hunger was on them and the sickness on Kit. They had to walk very slowly. When they had put a couple of miles of the journey past them, Kit was forced to stop. She was not able to walk any farther. A neighbour came across them. Drink and some little bit of food was given to them, but fear would not allow anyone to give them shelter since they were only just after coming out of the poorhouse and the evil sickness was on the woman. Patrick only lifted the woman onto his back and pushed on north-westwards for the cabin.

The poor man himself was weak enough. It would have been hard on him to put the journey by him without having any load. With the load, he was often forced to stop and to leave his load down on the ditch of the road for a while. But whatever weariness was on him, he continued to put that journey by him. He did not part with his load. He reached the cabin. The cabin was cold and empty before him, without fire nor heat.

The morning after, some neighbour came to the cabin. He went inside. He saw the pair there and they both dead, and the feet of the woman in Patrick's bosom, as if he had been trying to warm them. It would seem that he had felt the weakness of death coming over Kit and her feet cold, and he put the feet into his own bosom to take the cold from them.

'He was a good, loyal, noble man!' some person might say, perhaps, 'and the deed he did was a noble one!'

It is true. But I will tell you this much. Thousands of deeds of the same kind were done in Ireland during that period, and nobody was one whit amazed at the excellence of the deeds. According to everyone, Patrick Buckley had only done a thing that any man, who was worth calling a Christian, would have done.

That little man-een, whose name was Michael O'Leary, was living in a cabin not far from that in which Patrick Buckley and his wife died. Black Michael was a nick-name they had on him. Cathleen Purcell was his wife's name. They had the full of the house of children. There wasn't as much as one word of English in themselves or in the children. The famine came hard on them. Tadhg was the name of their eldest son. He saw his father and mother growing weak with the hunger, and the youngest member of the family stretched dead in a corner of the cabin. At nightfall, he took an axe and a knife with him and out he went. He went into the cowhouse of one of the neighbours and he killed a beast. He took some of the skin from it, stripping the amount of meat he wanted to bring with him. He took away the two hind quarters and came home. They all had a good meal that night. When the hunger had been taken from them, Tadhg took out the body that was in the corner, and he made a hole out in the garden and put the body in it.

When the morning came, the people who owned the cow rose and found the cow dead out in the shed, with its two hind quarters gone. The owner went to Macroom and got a search warrant. He had an idea where the meat was brought. He and whatever law-officer he had with him came to Black Michael's cabin. The bones and some of the meat was found. Tadhg was taken prisoner and brought to Macroom and put into prison. When the time came for it, he was tried. He was sentenced without much hesitation and transported. I never heard any report since then of what happened him afterwards nor of what end befell him.

Michael and Cathleen and those of the family who still lived left the cabin and took to the roads.

Some days after they had gone away, a neighbour was going past the cabin. He saw a hound, with something in his mouth, in the garden; the hound threw down the thing he had in his mouth and ran away. The neighbour came over and he nearly fell with the shock and the horror when he saw that it was a person's hand that the dog had in his mouth! Tadhg hadn't made the hole deep enough before he had put the body down into it.

The neighbour found a box or something of the sort. He took the rest of the body from the hole, and brought the box to the nearest graveyard and buried it. It was no cause for wonder at that time to see a person going by himself to a graveyard and a coffin with him in his cart, or on the back of two cattle if he hadn't got a horse nor a cart.

That was the way things were then, ugly and hateful and loathsome, round about the area in which I was reared. I understand that the story was exactly the same all about the whole of Ireland. And, to make matters altogether worse, it was not really by the will of God that things were so. It was that way because of the will of people. There was sent out from Ireland that year as much—no! twice as much—corn as would have nourished every person living in the country. The harbours of Ireland were full of ships and the ships full of Irish corn: they were leaving the harbours while the people were dying with the hunger throughout the land.

'Why wasn't the corn kept here?' someone will say, perhaps.

It was not kept because it had to be sold to pay the rent, it and the butter and the meat, and every other bit of produce from the land, excepting the potatoes. The blackness took away the potatoes and then there was no food left for people to eat.

Someone will say, perhaps: 'Why wasn't a law made to protect the people from the injustice that forced the people to sell the corn and not to keep anything for themselves to eat?'

I'm sorry for your want of knowledge! 'A law to protect the people,' you say? *Airiú*, if you had spoken to the gentlemen of England at that time of a law to protect the people, they would have said you were mad.

It was not at all for the protection of the people that the English made laws that time. To crush the people down and to plunder them, to put them to death by famine and by every other kind of injustice—that's why the English made laws in those days. It is a strange story, but the English had a sort of proverb then. Here's the proverb: 'To give the tenant his rights is an injustice to the landlord'.

NOTES TO CHAPTER VI

1. Cecil Woodham-Smith's *'The Great Hunger'* (Hamish Hamilton and Four Square Books) is now generally accepted as the authoritative study of the 1845–48 Famine.
2. See Appendix 8.

CHAPTER VII

THE SCHOOL AT CARRIGANIMMY

WHEN I was about thirteen years of age, a schoolhouse was built east in Carriganimmy. Until then, it was at home that myself and the rest of my parents' family had the school. We would work on the small farm during the day (those of us who were able to do anything in the form of work); when the night would come, my mother would light a candle on the table, put us sitting around, give us the books and teach us our lessons.

Her teaching was far better than the teaching which used to be given to the children in the schools. Nevertheless, it was thought— and no wonder—that the teaching in the schools had to be better than hers.

The school at Carriganimmy was opened. A teacher, by the name of Cormac Lucy, was put into it. I was sent there to school. I well recall the first day that I went. Cormac could not decide on which class in the school he would put me into. Some of the knowledge I had very well, but there was more of it which I hadn't got at all. I was able to read the books that they had beautifully, far better than the best boy there. But then there were other things of which I had never come across any mention. What used he do but put me in a low position for a while and then in a high one: he used put me teaching for a while and then learning. He had had a good education himself and he had a good head—but he was very hot-tempered.

I was amazed when, in that school, I saw for the first time young people learning, reading and speaking words and then telling what their meanings were, while they hadn't got the slightest idea as to the meaning of the words or the meaning of the meaning! There was no danger of anything of that sort at home with us. There was no danger that any word was left without the meaning being given to us, so that we used understand both word and meaning.

I recall how things were with me, at times, when we would be studying our lessons and sitting at the school-desks. I would be sitting and the other boys, some of whom were much bigger and older than me, would be collected about me so that they'd have me smothered, and I answering their questions, telling them the meanings of the words in the lesson. They'd be wondering where I got all the knowledge, I'd be wondering how anyone could be without that knowledge. Cormac used see us, but he would not let on that he saw. He knew that good was being done and he was satisfied.

That things were like that among the boys and myself was no wonder at all. They were never given the opportunity which had been given to me to get the knowledge of those English words. They would never hear a word at home but of Gaelic or broken English. The English which they had in the books was the same to them as Greek.

We all had fine Gaelic. Cormac himself had it beautifully. The yard, which was out in front of the schoolhouse, was full of big rocks of stones. I saw two men one day, breaking the stones so as to bring them out of the place. Cormac was talking to the men. They were talking in Gaelic. There was one stone there and, it was so hard, the men had failed to break it. It was three or four feet in thickness in every way and you'd swear it was as round as a football. The men were examining it to see if they could find a place, where a good, strong blow of the sledge-hammer would split it. They were failing. Cormac took the sledge. A strong, hard, vigorous young man he was at the time.

'Stand back from it!' says he.

He took a swing out of the sledge-hammer and he struck as good a blow as there was in his wrists and body to strike. I was looking at him—you'd think that the sledge rose off the stone with more vigour than it had come down upon it! I think that the timber shook in Cormac's hand so that it gave him pins-and-needles. He threw away the sledge and put the hand in his pocket.

Said one of the men to him: 'A feather is lighter than it, Cormac!'

In Carriganimmy, the chapel[1] was beside the school, and, when we were to learn catechism, we used all go from the school into the chapel. There was only a very little English spoken in the chapel. There used to be twice as many learning catechism there as used to be learning lessons in the school, and there was no danger that every word of the teaching would not be understood in the chapel.

I recall a day when we were all together inside in the chapel. The priest was there, teaching the catechism, and he was very good at it. He spoke Gaelic eloquently; myself and the other boys would often go barefoot over the hills on a Sunday morning to the chapel in which he was to say Mass, so that we would hear the sermon in Gaelic that he'd give, the sermon would be that good.

He was there on the day I'm speaking about. There was, at the least, up to a couple of hundred people learning there. At some point during the time, a very small, little lad, with a folded shawl under his arm, came boldly in the door towards us. He walked very slowly up to us, with his two eyes on the priest. The priest thought that perhaps he was shy or afraid of him, so he spoke quietly and mildly to him.

'Yes, little man,' the priest said, 'what do you want?'

'One of those little girls, Father,' said the little lad, with neither shyness nor fear in his speech or voice. He spoke as boldly as if he was as great and as strong as the priest himself. We all burst out laughing. The priest himself let out a roar of laughter. That didn't make the little lad in any way uneasy.

'And what do you want with that shawl?' said the priest.

'To put it round her, Father.'

It's then we had the fun and we in fits of laughing. While this was going on, one of the girls hopped out from the others and she ran up to the boy, snapped the shawl from him, threw it around her and out the door with her. He looked after her.

'Go east to Maulnahorna, Peg.' he said, 'and tell them that we'll be making butter on Monday and that we'll have the mowers on Tuesday.'

When he had said that much, he walked boldly up to us and stood in amongst us.

The memory of that lad has never since left my mind. Long afterwards, when the child and his talk used to come up in my mind and I used be reviewing the story, I would compare that child, as he was then, with the way he would be some time later if he had gone to a foreign school,[2] and if he had learned the type of English which was in these schools. That time, he was not nervous but self-confident, able to look anybody straight in the face and ready with an answer when asked a question. He looked the priest between the two eyes when he was speaking to him. He was bold, without being bad-mannered.

I never saw him since then. But I often saw people of his sort. And I know right well that, if he were to spend some time in a foreign school and learned the kind of English which was in these schools, it would not be long until the resoluteness would leave his eyes and his heart and that, if he had to come into a chapel with a shawl under his arm and if some priest were to question him about it, it is how he would be tittering instead of giving an answer and cringing instead of standing erect. Instead of being bold without being bad-mannered, it is how he would be bad-mannered without being bold.[3]

There were in the parish two or three women, each with a couple of girls learning catechism in the chapel. Gaelic wouldn't suit these women at all. Catechism had to be taught in English to their families. Out of the two hundred, there were four or five trying to learn catechism through English. I was put teaching them. I was very small and they were very big. I recall well the work I had to do with them, trying to put the words into their heads and failing completely. Firstly, they couldn't say the words. When I would tell them to say 'Resurrection', they could only answer 'Rerusection' or something like that. Then, when I would give them the meaning, I would realize that it would not go into their heads at all. Lastly, when I would give them the particular meaning, not heeding the word, they could grasp it—but my best efforts could not get them to take in both word and meaning together. They might know 'Resurrection' and 'to rise from the dead', but they could never understand that the two things were one and the same. Then, when I would tell them that the two things had the same meaning, i.e. *'Aiséirighe ár Slánuightheora'*, their eyes would light up and they would laugh.

Some years later, the school was seven times worse than that. Most of the young people were learning catechism through English, but without one word of Gaelic. Then they had neither 'Resurrection', nor 'rising from the dead', nor *'Aiséirighe ár Slánuightheora'!*

I don't think that so great an injustice was ever done to young people's minds in any part of the world as was done to the youth of Ireland, when this type of teaching, which left them with neither English nor Gaelic, was forced on them. When I was at school in Carriganimmy, up to three score years ago, that injustice was beginning. Only that I had such a firm grasp of both English and Gaelic, things would have gone badly with me.

If I had but Gaelic only now, there would be no notice taken of me, however well or badly I might have it; and if I had but English only, however well or badly I might have that, I could not make use of it to cultivate the Gaelic.

NOTES TO CHAPTER VII

1. In Irish, the normal word for a Roman Catholic church is *'séipéal'*, which corresponds to 'chapel' (as opposed to *'eaglais'*, meaning 'church'), because of the limitations imposed on Catholics in regard to church building prior to emancipation. For the same reason, the Dissenters' or Nonconformists' places of worship were also called 'chapels'. In many parts of Ireland, a Protestant is still said to go 'to church', and a Catholic 'to Chapel'.

2. i.e. a National School. See Appendix 9.

3. Is there any better depiction of the change in the national character than in Canon Sheehan's fine novel, *The Graves at Kilmorna*?

CHAPTER VIII

THREE BLACK BALLS

THERE's a good length in the distance from Liscarrigane to Carriganimmy, and a rough, troublesome way it is. When the weather used be wet and cold, I would have to stay at home—and that used be often enough. My father (the blessing of God on his soul) realized that a lot of my time was going by unfruitfully. At that time in Macroom, there was a school of high repute—and whose master was held in high repute. I think that perhaps Cormac Lucy had been talking with my father and told him that it would be a great pity not to give me my chance in the Macroom school.

About the same time, another legal wrangle arose between the tenants of the townland and the master. One of the tenants held his rent back, when it ought to have been paid. Broderick was the name of the agent over them. He was a villainous rogue. He had let the man, who was holding back, go on until he had a good amount to pay; he did this so that he could come down on them all with the demand. He was hoping that they would refuse it; he knew that some of them were hardly able to get their own share of the rent together never mind this further demand. If they refused, the lease would be broken and he would throw them all out, get a raise in rent for the master and get a fine profit out of every little farm he'd give to a new tenant.

The tenants united and went to law. They united, but they found it difficult to do so. They used to come to our house to take council, because it was the nearest for all. I well recall a day they were gathered at home. They spent the whole day talking and they failed to settle on what was the right thing for them to do.

'It's night now,' said one of them, 'It's as well for us to go home and come again next Wednesday. We have plenty of time yet to talk to our solicitor.'

Sean O'Leary, a son of old Jeremiah O'Leary, was listening to this talk. (There wasn't a word of English spoken at that council.)

'Yes!' said Sean O'Leary. 'Ye've spent the whole day here talking and ye've done nothing. No more than when ye came in here this morning, ye haven't agreed on what is to be done. ye will go away home now and ye will come back next Wednesday. Sean Lucy will come here, and each eye of him like a watch. Michael O'Leary will come here, and you'd think every word out of him was worth five pounds. Barnaby will come here, and, sure, you'd think he was Socrates. Ye'll all come and every one of ye will keep his own little mind to himself, and ye'll come to no agreement that day, no more than ye've done today. The time'll slip away from ye until it's too late to talk to any solicitor. Then, Broderick and Saunders will be down on the napes of all your necks, and they with the power to take whatever twist they like out of ye.'

By the time he had come to a stop, they were all putting their souls out laughing. They agreed to go on the spot and talk with the solicitor, and to put the law into motion to protect themselves. They beat the master in the law-case. The rent of the man, who was in arrears was paid, but the farm he had was given to them, until they had their share out of it.

When that much wrangling had been put behind him, my father settled on sending me (for a while, at any rate) to school down in Macroom. It was a very difficult thing for him to do. I was just beginning to be able to do some work, and he needed the help, no matter how trivial it was. But he himself always had a desire for learning, and he wanted to give some piece of it to his son, however it should come to him.

I had often been in Macroom before. I recall that I was there once, a good while before this, and that I was standing at the head of the bridge, at the bottom of the Road of the Whisps. I was looking over at the castle, which is across on the far side of the bridge. I saw, facing the castle on the east side of the little street called Castle Street, some big house with high, fortified walls around it, and three slender, high poles sticking up out of it—and at the very top of each pole was something like a little, black ball. At the time, I hadn't got the slight idea as to the meaning of the sticks and the small ball but, long afterwards, I was told that the poles were spikes of iron and that the three small balls were three skulls. These were the heads of the men who were hung because of Malachy Duggan. They were McCarthys, three brothers, Cormac, Callaghan and Tadhg. Malachy compelled Cormac to shoot Bob Hutchinson,[1] then he swore informations against him. Then he became afraid that one of the two brothers would wreak vengeance on him on account of the swearing, so what he did was to swear against the three brothers together. The three were hanged at the same time. Their heads were put up there on those high, slender spikes and left for many years. I saw them and I standing at the head of the bridge that day. Not too long afterwards, they were taken down; the gentry were ashamed to leave them there any more. Ever afterwards, that deed and others which he was to do later were repeatedly flung into Malachy's face and into the face of everyone of his relatives. Nobody wished to have anything to do with them, the whole countryside had such an abhorrence of them. That, however, was a great injustice because the majority of the family were decent, honest people, as decent and as honest as any other tribe of people in the district.[2]

Jeremiah Toohey, father of Maura Toohey (that is, my grandmother's father), was living at Glenday. There's a stream between the place on which he lived and the other farm west of it. This farm was to be let. Who should come and take it but a man by name of Daniel Duggan, a near relative of Malachy's. Jeremiah Toohey was raging to have it said that anyone of that evil class would be so close to him. Dan Duggan was not long living west of the stream when, one fine summer's morning, he and Jerry met.

'God and Mary to you, Jeremiah Toohey!' Dan said.

Jerry turned his back to him and struck on past him without speaking. Time went by. It wasn't long until Jerry noticed that he had a very good neighbour, very peaceable, very honourable, in Daniel, whatever relationship he had with Malachy. One year exactly from the day Dan had greeted Jerry, the pair met each other again.

'God and Mary to you, Daniel Duggan!' Jerry said.

But Dan turned his back to him and struck on past him, exactly as Jerry had done that first day. One year exactly from that day, they met a third time.

'Oh, God and Mary and Patrick to you!' answered Dan, exactly as he would have said it if it had been at that minute that Jerry had greeted him. If Jerry had taken a year to speak, it took Dan a year to answer. The pair laughed heartily and they were very close from that out.

When the time came for it, and the opportunity, I was sent down to the school, that a man by name of Michael Wall had, in Macroom. The school was so good that scholars used come to it from the entire countryside round about. I well recall that the master was every bit as bewildered as Cormac Lucy in Carriganimmy had been about which class in the school it would be right to put me into. I had some of the knowledge too well for any low class; and without portion of it good enough for an upper class. But an agreement was reached. I recall, besides, that when we would be studying our lessons in the reading books, that a crowd of the boys would be about me, crushing in on me from every side, each one with his book, and I telling them how to say the words and what was their meaning. It wouldn't be right, however, to give me any credit because of that. They were never given the knowledge on books and on English literature that I had been given at home.

On the Road of Whisps, in the house of a man by the name of Sean O'Shea, I used to lodge. Himself and my father knew each other. He was a generous, good-hearted man. He never took one halfpenny of payment for my lodgings and I was there a good while, a couple of years or three. I used to go up home to Liscarrigane every Saturday. There's a son of the same Sean O'Shea's living in the same street now, and his name is also Sean O'Shea, and he is as solid and as respectable a man as is to be found in the barony.

After I had spent some time in Michael Wall's school in Macroom—I don't rightly recall now how long it was—the master spoke to my father. They walked up the Road of Whisps, shoulder to shoulder, talking.

'It's a great pity entirely,' Michael said, 'not to give that lad an opportunity of learning languages. I have nothing more to teach him—that is, nothing that would be of any advantage to him. And the amount that I've taught him,' said he, 'what advantage is that to him now if it's up at home you're thinking of keeping him?'

My father told him that he had always and ever heard me saying that I would prefer more than anything else to be a priest.

'But what is the good of talking about it,' he said, 'when I haven't a hope of standing the losses in making him a priest!'

'The losses won't be as great at all as you think,' said the other man. 'There's a Latin School here in Macroom now. You could send him to that school and you would only have to pay a pound in the quarter-year. At the end of a couple of years or three, from the knowledge I've got of him, I'd go bail that he would have as much Latin and Greek learned as would bring him into Maynooth College. Then, you wouldn't have another halfpenny's losses with him, and, at the end of six or seven years (if it is God's will that his health would stand up) he'd be coming home to you as a priest. He has the power of reflexion required for learning—and the ambition. If you keep him at home, you'll have nothing for it. He'll never grow very big. He'll never have the bulk nor the strength that labouring on a farm calls for, and, if he had itself, you have enough help in the rest of the family.'

The upshot of the story was that my father agreed to put me learning Latin.

NOTES TO CHAPTER VIII

1. Evidently Whiteboy trouble. See Appendix 10.
2. The folk-memory in this respect is surprisingly long-living. I recall an incident from my youth, some twenty-five or so years ago: a schoolfellow in a Co Sligo town, where we lived, had done some prank of more than usual mischief. 'It's the breed of him!' I overheard a man comment, with a spit. The boy's family, strangers to the town, did not stay there too long; people said, when they had gone, 'It's no loss!' That family was unfortunate enough to bear the name of Carey, that of the man who had turned informer on the Invincibles more than fifty years earlier. To escape opprobrium, many families in Co Tipperary and in Co. Limerick are said to have changed their names from Carey to Carew following the infamous informations. For the best insight into the subject, one reaches automatically for Canon Sheehan's novel, *Glenanaar*.

CHAPTER IX

MACROOM SCHOOL AND COLMAN'S COLLEGE

A SMALL man-een named McNally had a Latin school on the far side of the bridge in Macroom, exactly at the foot of the castle. You would go across the bridge in the direction of the castle, when you'd be at the far end of the bridge, exactly at the end of the railing, you would turn into your right and go down a couple of steps of stairs or three. Then you'd see the door in front of you. You'd knock on the door. It would be opened for you. You'd go into the hall. Another door, on your right-hand side, would be opened for you. You'd go into a room. You would see inside before you six or seven lads, sitting at a table, learning, and the master at the head of the table, and he teaching. You'd see a window inside opposite the door. You'd look out that window and see, slap up against the bottom of the window, the river, the Solan, going past the window eastwards and into the eyes of the bridge, grandly and easily, wide and calm.

Inside in that room, with my left shoulder to the window, it was that I laid my eyes for the first time ever on those three small, wretched words, '*hic, haec, hoc*'. You've only got three of them there, but there are ten and twenty of them altogether in the declining of that one little word. I had plenty of experience of them afterwards, but, the first time that I ever set out to learn them, they broke the heart in me. If I had been told at first what was their meaning, my mind might have gained some grip on them; but I was not told. It was a strange kind of teaching: taking in the words by heart at first, before any opportunity was given to the judgement to handle them at all! And, you'd think, anyone with any sense ought to know that it would be far easier to take in my heart a thing that is understood than it would be before it is understood. But, in truth, much more learning without understanding was certainly done in that small room than learning with understanding.

But I wasn't too long in the room when I was working away at 'Caesar'. I recall that one day I was not at school—I can't recall now what reason kept me away—but I was inside in Sean O'Shea's house in the evening and I working away on 'Caesar' at my best. I came to the words '*propterea quod*'. I knew '*propterea*' was the same as 'because'. 'And,' said I to myself, 'what is the "*quod*" for?' I was stuck. I couldn't make out at all what business *'quod'* had in that place. Who should come into me but the master. He came to see what had kept me from school that day. I told him and he was satisfied—he had been afraid that I was sick. Over to the book with me.

'Look here, sir,' said I in English, 'what is the meaning of this *"propterea quod"*?'

'Oh,' he said, ' *"propterea quod"* is "because".'

'But,' I said, 'what is *"quod"*?'

'Oh,' he said, 'that is quite simple. *"Quod"* is "because"; *"propterea quod"* is "because".' And he looked at me as much as if to say 'You must be very stupid not to see that simple matter.'

I didn't go farther into the matter with him, of course. I had *'propterea'* for 'because'; I had *'quod'* for 'because'; and I had *'propterea quod'* for 'because'. And if that wouldn't satisfy me, what would?

The master reminded me of a story I had heard a long time before from Seán O'Leary, the man who had said to Seán Lucy that each of his eyes were 'like a watch'.

Long ago, when the French fleet came into Bantry Bay, there were two cowherds some place behind Bantry. One was called Jerry, the other Dan. The two farms, on which they were herding, were bordering each other. The pair would meet often on the two sides of the border ditch and they'd be yarning. No sooner were the French inside in Bantry Bay than the story quickly spread out over the countryside round about. The two herds met.

'God and Mary to you, Jer.'

'God and Mary and Patrick to you, Dan.'

'Have you anything new, Jer?'

'By my word, I have, Dan, and it isn't a good story but the worst of bad ones.'

'*Ach*! God be with us! Jer, what kind of story is it?'

'That there is a great *invasion* altogether coming.' (They were, of course, talking in Gaelic, but Jerry used the English word, 'invasion'.)

'And who told you, Jer, that it was coming?'

'Everybody has it.'

'*Ach*! may God help us! What'll people do at all?'

'I don't know in the world what they'll do. They'll be in a bad way, I'm afraid.'

'And whisper, Jer. When is it coming?'

'*Ambasa* but it's on top of you, *a mhic-ó*!'

'A great *invasion*! God be with us and Mary!'

'A great *invasion*, exactly, the greatest *invasion* that has come to Ireland yet!'

'And whisper, Jer. As you know, I'm not the most well-up person in this sort of thing. What kind of thing—do you understand me?—is this great *invasion*?'

'Well, Dan, it's an *invasion*—do you understand? That is to say, *"invasion"*. It's only as if a person were to say *"invasion"*, do you know?'

'Oh, I know now, Jer.'

Seán O'Leary would let a roar of laughter out of him when he'd have this story told, and everybody listening to him, sure, would do the same. The master explained *'propterea quod'* to me in exactly the same way—'It's only as if you'd say "because" there, do you know?'

'I know now,' said I, and I left it at that.

The master had a great craving for the puff of the pipe. While we'd be struggling with *hic, haec, hoc,* the poor master'd be drinking his pipe. The poor man was heavy on it. He'd be drawing on the pipe and the smoke going throughout the room until we could hardly see each other, never mind read a book. At last, he went away from the village altogether, and left us there.

There was another Latin school at Macroom at the same time. It was up in Massy's Road and there was a man, by name of Terence Golden, teaching it. When McNally had gone, we all went up to Golden. I think I spent a half-year in that school.

At that time exactly, Colman's College was opened in Fermoy. I—and many like me—could not go to the college, as I would have had to pay ten and twenty pounds per year there.

When Colman's opened, some of the priests throughout the countryside were complaining severely on the injustice this college would do to boys who had the intellectual ability but whose fathers hadn't got the capital. Because of the complaint, the Bishop, Dr William Keane, made an arrangement. He arranged that any boy, who had excellent intellectual ability but who had not got the money, would have to be taken free into Colman's College. That satisfied many of the priests. There were some who weren't satisfied. They said to themselves that the arrangement wouldn't be of much advantage. There was no money other than that the boys paid to keep the college going, therefore, it would be possible to accept only a truly small number of boys free, however much intellectual ability they might have. A lot of the priests said it would be better to let every boy procure his learning at any school he choose and to give the place in Maynooth College to the best boy. More of them said that that would be no good at all. That it would be a great mind-opener, and an eye-opener, for any boy to give him the opportunity of spending some time in a public school near home before he would go into Maynooth College. That, outside of that, when there'd be a competitive examination between the boys from the country schools and the boys of Colman's College, the college boys would win, no matter what ability the country boys would have. Against this, it was said that the teaching in the country schools (or in some of them, at any rate) was better than that which was to be had inside in the college, even after ten-and-twenty pounds in the year had been paid for it.

There was a parish priest in Donoughmore, ten miles north east of Macroom, and he was fixed in that opinion. To show that he was right, he took Terence Golden from Macroom and opened a school in Donoughmore for him; he put him teaching the languages there.

That left me once more on the *seachrán*. But there was a man of the Sullivans, from Kerry, teaching school in Kanturk. There was also a man, by the name of Thomas O'Leary, living at Derrynamona, about three miles west of Kanturk; he and my mother were the children of two brothers. I went north to school in Kanturk and I would come to Derrynamona every night, to the house of Thomas O'Leary. I spent, I suppose, a year or a year and a half at that school.

The school was fairly good for a while. There were a lot of scholars coming there, but the master had no assistance. Often, it is how everybody was teaching himself as well as he was able. Out in an old stable, our school was. When winter came, it was desperately cold. When the weather would be cold, we would have a fire—but there was no chimney in the stable. There was a hole in the wall behind the fire, however. This did fine—while the wind was going west through it. But when the wind was blowing from the west, we used be smothered with the smoke—and the smoke was far worse than the cold. In fact, it is how we used to have both cold and smoke at once, for the fire was but a poor one.

At last it was realized everywhere that there was no good for country schools going into competition with the college in Fermoy. Things were then arranged in the college so that a boy could come there and not have to pay the ten-and-twenty pounds; he could come and take lodgings in the town, and go into the college every day. He would only have to pay six pounds in the year for his schooling then, and he could keep himself as cheaply as he was able.

Bear in mind, reader, that the people of Ireland had a very hard life then. The man, who had a farm of land, had to be working from darkness to darkness to make the rent and to feed and clothe himself and whatever family was in his care. He, who decided on giving an education to a son, had to bring double the work out of himself and the rest of the family in order to get this individual ahead. Because of that, the boy, who went to Colman's College and took lodgings in the town for himself, would have to feed himself without any liberality, or otherwise he would be doing an injustice to his people at home, who were working so hard to get him ahead.

As the boys were leaving the country schools, these were (and no wonder) losing ground and deteriorating. My father realized that it was no good keeping me any longer in Kanturk. He decided that it would be better for him to send me as a day-scholar to Colman's College. He did just that. I spent a year lodging in the town and going into the college every single day.[1] When the end of the year and the competitive examination came (to see who would get to go to Maynooth College), I entered for it like everyone else.

The boys, who were living in the college, had a big advantage over those who were outside in lodgings, for the residents used to be taught every evening. Three score and four of the boys went in for that examination. When the test was made, it was found that I was the fourth person; there were only three better than me. But that was no good to me, for there were only three vacant places in Maynooth that year. My father went and spoke to the Bishop and reminded him of the arrangement that was made when the College was opened. Because of that arrangement, the Bishop gave me a free place in the College for the coming year, and when the examination came again, I got to Maynooth. In the year of the Lord a thousand eight hundred, three score and one that happened.

NOTES TO CHAPTER IX

1. Four years later, an orphan boy named Patrick Sheehan entered St Colman's. He was to follow Peter O'Leary to Maynooth. Later still, he was appointed parish priest in Doneraile, a couple of years after Canon O'Leary, who had been curate there, was appointed parish priest in Castlelgons. There are many interesting parallels in the careers of Canon Sheehan, internationally-famous novelist, and of Canon O'Leary, the first great name in modern Gaelic writing. Paradoxically, their trails do not often seem to have crossed.

CHAPTER X

MAYNOOTH

In 1861, I went down to Maynooth College to spend the appointed period preparing to be a priest.

It was the rule of the College at the time that a person had to spend eight, seven or six years there, learning the arts that were necessary in order that he would have the right knowledge so as to be made a priest. When the youths would enter, they would undergo an examination, despite the examination that the Bishops outside had given them. If the examination showed that it was not necessary for a youth to spend eight years in there, a year would be remitted; and if the examination showed that it was not necessary for him to spend the seven years inside, two years' work would be remitted. I was let off the two years. That was of great benefit to me, as the air of the place is very severe on the health of the boys who go there from the country. Whatever in the world it was, they found it severe. I don't know if it has improved since or has not. Fine, big, strong boys went in the same year as I did. No sooner had they spent a year inside than they were quite emaciated. When they would go home during the summer season, they would put on weight again and their strength would come back. But the weight and strength would leave them again when they were some time after coming back. When the end of the period was passed and they were going out as fully-finished priests, their bones would be bare enough on them all, especially those who had been reared in the country. Those, who had been reared in the villages or towns, would have been nowhere near as much affected by the place. They wouldn't have, from the onset, the same strength as the young men, who had come in from the country, but, whatever amount of strength they had, they would keep it during the period. In comparison with the country boys, they were weak and insignificant at the onset; but coming near the end of the period, they were in much the same shape, whereas all the vigour, or almost all, would have been plundered from the country boys.

Splendid boys used to come from County Tipperary. I recall one who came the year I entered. He was over six feet in height and he was so well-built, so well-proportioned that you would think it fine to be looking at him and he walking with his comrades. They were all quite big and well-built, but I would say that he was a head and half a neck clear above them all. He had astonishing strength. He and three others were playing a game of handball one day. They all knew him for strength. The three others whispered among themselves that they would grab him and knock him. I was watching the play myself: there was never much good in me for any athletics of the sort. It wasn't long until I saw the three closing in on him. Two of them had their arms round his middle and the third had a hold of his knees. The strong man bent his knees and he let himself down until he had the pair on top fast under his armpits and a hold with his two hands on the hindquarters of the bottom man. Then, he straightened himself up and he took the three of them with him clear off the ground and he walked around the court with them. When he let them loose, they had to sit down for a while to come to themselves after the squeezing he had given them. But he had been only laughing all the time he was carrying them! And they were all three active, strong and capable men!

'Yes,' he said, when he let them go, 'have ye had enough of sport?'

'We thought,' said one of them, 'that we'd have it to say that we'd knocked you. But what did you squeeze me so much for? I've a pain in my back and up to the top of my head yet!'

The big man was sorry when he saw the state they were in and he was making apologies to them, saying that he didn't feel himself putting that strength into the squeezes—that he thought he'd only given them a squeeze that would keep a hold on them while lifting them from the ground.

'By dad,' said the third person, 'if you had squeezed me any more, you had me killed!'

A couple of years afterwards, I saw that man and he had very little strength. The air and the food of the place adversely affected him, and he collapsed. He had to go home. He was too far gone, however, before he went home. He wasn't long in the house with his people when he went to his eternal home, may it turn out for his good!

I said that the air of the place affected him. It did, but that was no wonder. The place is too low and the canal, that goes west through the middle of the country, runs outside the wall of the College, and the mist from the canal dampens the air so that it is unhealthy to a person's chest, and there stimulates all kinds of chest diseases.

But I also said that the food affected him—this was a much more surprising affliction. The finest mutton, that any human ever tasted, is given, or used to be given to us, at any rate. Not a fault could be found with it, no more than fault could be found with the bread we used to get. But however fine the meat and the bread was, they didn't do much good to some of us. Those of us, who had come in from the country, were not used to meat. Meal, potatoes and milk was all we used to have at home; meat was not to be had but seldom, or, perhaps, very seldom. Then, when we'd go to the College, all that could be got was meat. We'd have left the fine, healthy air and the food, on which we were reared, behind us outside. The food inside was very good—but it wasn't on such we were reared and we were not used to it. It didn't suit us. The signs were on it, for, when we used come home on the summer holidays, our mothers would hardly recognize us, we would be looking so bare, pale and starved.

While we would be at home, we'd have our fill once more of the food on which we were reared, oatmeal bread and wheaten bread from the mill, hen-eggs and duck-eggs, sweet milk and thick milk and buttermilk, the potatoes and the butter taken fresh from the churn, the bit of bacon now and again. That's the food that would do us good. We'd put on weight again at a great rate—and the chubby cheeks; and the strength and vigour would come again into us so that, when the three months' holidays would be spent and we would go back to the College, the superiors would hardly recognise us and we would hardly recognise each other.

I put the first year by me without any failing coming on my strength, although I was very bare when I came home in the summer. I went back in the autumn, fine and strong. I wasn't long inside, however, when my stomach began to play up on me. From that on. I had to spend a good deal of my time in the infirmary and I was only able to give as much attention to my studies as would bring me past each examination, as it came. I would have the grand, long three months in the summer and that would nearly cure the amount of damage done in the rest of the year.

During the six years I put in there in the College, I used often reflect on those colleges which they had in Ireland in ancient times. Neither teachers nor students had any fine, big, slated houses. It's how everybody had his own small house—nice and well-sheltered with a good thatched roof on it, and no furniture in it except for a table and a bed and a couple of chairs, perhaps, and the hearth. We are told that it was normal for the students to be going round about the neighbourhood 'gathering' milk for themselves. They hadn't got the grand walls round them like we had, but I reckon that their health was better than that of the Maynooth College students, at the time I knew the place at any rate. Perhaps, things are better with them now.

CHAPTER XI

GAELIC IN DANGER

DURING the time I had been at home, when I had no acquaintance with or knowledge of any others but the neighbours about me in the parishes of Clondrohid and Ballyvourney, there never came a day that I thought of Gaelic as being in danger. But when I went into the college and got to know the boys who were raised in other places, and when I found out that they hadn't got one word of Gaelic, I was dumb with amazement. It was only then it struck me that Gaelic was on the way out: it would be going like the old people were going and the young ones coming. A generation would arise with the two tongues, Gaelic and English together, and a generation would arise after that again and these would not have one word of Gaelic. When I was struck with this thought, an extreme sense of isolation came over me, and so, too, did sorrow and shame. I would almost have preferred to go to some foreign country, to spend and end my life there, than to be in Éire and it turning into a foreign country. In my opinion, it would not be Éire at all when there wouldn't be a word of Gaelic spoken in it.

The result of my reflection, sorrow and isolation was that I decided, whatever any other person might do, I would not let my own amount of the language go to nothing. On the spot, I began to say 'Mary's Crown'[1] in Gaelic, like we used to do at home and north at Derrynamona while I was there. This kept me from getting out of practice with the language. I began, also, to read it for myself from the books I'd get in the college library,[2] and I used to write down anything that appealed to me in a little pocket-book which I had.

This much I did, but, at the same time, I was constantly asking myself if there was any use in the business, or if my best efforts could put a stop to the blight that had come on the language. There were many things before my eyes which were impressing on my mind that my work was silly. Most of the other boys, when they saw what I was at, would do nothing but shake their heads, laugh and give me up as a bad job.[3] More and more, I thought that perhaps I was making a mistake. I'd see everyone attempting through English to improve and perfect himself in knowledge, capability and attainment. What could one single person do?

By degrees, my enthusiasm slackened and I turned my face to
those affairs which had to do with the work of the College in
English, Latin and French. I continued, however, with my 'Crown
of Mary' in Gaelic when I'd be going to bed. Now and again, I
used to write down in my notebook little bits of Gaelic which would
cross my path. I recall how, one day, I was looking at a Gaelic book
in the library and saw this little poem on the border of a page:

O Dove in the dark fort, there with your sad tune,
Crumbles the ceremonial court beneath you in gloom:
By great Ua Róig's rampart, on his assembly-mound,
No companies, no unchecked mirth, no cauldrons found.![4]

I realized that the poet was looking over at some old, broken-
down castle and saw a pigeon standing high on top of it, crying
Coo-oo! Coo-oo! I knew the poet felt that the pigeon was 'groaning
and sighing' while keening the nobility who had possessed the
castle before it became an old ruin.

While it was impressing itself on my mind that it was nothing but
a waste of time to attempt to do anything to put a stop to the blight
that was taking Gaelic from this world, I saw in some book what
Eugene O'Curry[5] had said about the work which he and his
contemporaries were doing: they were gathering and explaining
the Old Irish, which was in the ancient manuscripts, so that, when
spoken Irish had disappeared, there would be some trace or
remnant of it left in Ireland.

'By the deer!' said I in my mind, 'if, when Gaelic was as alive as it
then was, these men were so certain it was dying and that they,
despite their intellectual ability, had no chance of saving it from
death, what would they say now, if they were alive to see how it was
gone from more than half the island? If they realized that there was
no chance of putting an end to the blight then, what would they say
to the person who reckoned there was a chance of ending it now!'[6]

The finish of my reflections was that I discontinued my efforts—
but, as I have said, I continued saying my 'Crown of Mary' in
Gaelic.

During this time, it happened that a group of students were
being taken together every evening in a big hall to learn—as was
proper, fitting and right for educated people—to read, write and
speak English. It came about that I was with that group. We had a
young priest from the Cork diocese in charge of the work.

When the end of the year came, an essay was assigned for us all to
write and there was an individual prize for the person who would

write the best one. The subject, on which we had to write the essay, was 'The Elizabethan Age of English Literature'.

The end of the year came. We all went into the big hall. There were six or seven Bishops up on the stage. I was given the individual prize. I had to read some of the essay in the presence of the Bishops.

I recall that, at the beginning of the essay, I treated of the literature of Greece and praised it; I treated of the literature of Rome and I praised that; I treated of other European literatures, French, German and Spanish, the types of literatures descended from Greek and Latin, and I praised them. Then I treated of the literature and authors of England in the time of Elizabeth, and I praised them both. It wasn't difficult for me to do so. I knew a lot of it well. I had had them at home. My mother—the blesssing of God on her soul!—had taken them south with her from Mullaroe.

That was precisely the part of the essay which was marked out for me to read before the Bishops. I read it in a loud voice and without nervousness.

One of the Bishops, who was sitting up in the centre, right in front of me, stood up when I had finished and he looked me in the two eyes.

'You did that much well, boy,' he said. 'You paid your visit round to them all. You praised the literature of Greece. You praised the literature of Rome. You praised the literatures of France and of Spain and of Germany. Then, you praised—and highly—the literature of England. And behold! Not as much as one word did you say about the literature of Ireland.'

He said much more which opened my eyes for me to the great mistake I had made, for the literature of Ireland was finer and more noble and more ancient than any of the other literatures I had named. While he was speaking, we were both looking straight into each other's eyes, squarely and steadfastly.

The man, who had thus reproached me in Maynooth College in front of the other Bishops, in front of the superiors, in front of the other collegians, was John MacHale, Archbishop of Tuam.[7] I confess from the heart that he rightly took my high notions from me. The exaggerated veneration for English, which had come over me, went away and the respect, which I had earlier for Gaelic, lit up in my heart again. Once more, I began to read and to study the Gaelic books in the library and to note down in my book the little pieces of poetry which appealed to me. When I'd come home on holidays, I'd be going here and there throughout the neighbourhood gathering songs and old sayings from old people who had such things. I recall that one day I went west to Togher, and I got from a little, old person, who was living beside Lackabbogig, the song they called *'An Bodach Beag Tóstalach'*. That song is in print now and there's *no need to write it down here. I also got 'An Giolla Ruadh'* from him—the song which put into my mind that account of the fairy music, which I have set down in *'Séadna'*.

NOTES TO CHAPTER XI

1. i.e. the Rosary.
2. In later years, he was to recall these manuscripts and was prompted to re-write in the Irish of his day nearly a dozen versions of old tales and histories. See Appendix 5.
3. For a few remarks on Maynooth College and the Irish language, see Appendix 11.
4. A choluim an cheoil bhrónaigh sa ndún dubh thall,

   Is doilbh an róimh nósmhar san fút go fann.

   Tulach Uí Róig mhórdha na múrtha meann

   Gan choire, gan spórt seolta, gan lúbadh lann!

The final phrase presents difficulties to the translator, and may be corrupt.
5. Eugene O'Curry (Eoghan Ó Comhraighe), one of the great names in the history of the last century. Born in Dunaha, near Carrigaholt in Co Clare in 1796, he lived in obscurity until he was almost middle-aged. It is often said that he was self-educated, but this is only true as regards his knowledge of English. By the standards of the time, his family were wealthy farming folk, so prosperous in fact that what was probably the remnants of a bardic school came under their patronage. Eugene's father was very well versed in the old learning and the boy had evidently a large collection of manuscript material at hand; he was to be the last in a centuries-old line of Gaelic scholarship. The conclusion of the Napoleonic Wars brought poverty and the family came to Limerick city. Eugene eventually became a warder in the lunatic asylum.

By a stroke of fortune, in 1834, he found himself on the staff of the Ordnance Survey of Ireland, working in the topographical and historical section with George Petrie and John O'Donovan, his own brother-in-law. Before long, his reputation was guaranteed; but the government abandoned the survey through fear of the national memories which the work was evoking.

In 1855, Cardinal Newman appointed him Professor of Irish History and Archaeology in the recently-formed Catholic University of Ireland. His lectures were published—the monumental works, *The Manuscript Materials of Ancient Irish History* and *Manners and Customs of the Ancient Irish*. His background and researches had given him such a vast knowledge of Irish literature that it is still probably true to say that no one since then has had such an all-round grasp of the subject. He, O'Donovan and Petrie are often quite rightly called 'The Nation-Builders'.

6. This was some 30 years before the advent of the Gaelic League, in whose efforts to restore Irish as the lnaguage of the country Canon O'Leary was to play such a prominent part.

7. Archbishop John MacHale was the first Irish prelate since Reformation times to have had his entire education in Ireland. The usual hedgeschool education was, in his case, supplemented by the teaching of English in his home and he also studied under a local Gaelic scholar and scribe. This latter and the brutal reprisals by the British following the '98 Rebellion helped to shape him into the greatest of the pro-Irish Bishops in the last century. After having spent some time at a Classical school, the Mayo man entered Maynooth; he was only 23 and not yet ordained when he was given a lectureship in theology. In 1820, he was appointed Professor of Theology and some years later became coadjutor to the Bishop of Killala. Already well-known from his letters to the press, he was a friend of O'Connell and a very active advocate of Catholic Emancipation.

The government did everything in its power to prevent his being appointed to the See of Tuam and in the event they were proved right as MacHale proved himself one who could never toe the British line. He attacked the government savagely during the great famine and opposed their educational schemes, especially those of the national schools and Queen's Colleges. On the other hand, he was a supporter of Repeal, Tenant Right and Tenant League movements.

There were a small number of bishops in the last century who did not neglect the Irish language in their dealings with the native-speakers of their flocks, but Dr MacHale was outstanding in this respect. He translated a cathechism, prayerbook, hymns and parts of scripture into the language. His translation of Homer's *Iliad* is a fine piece of work but the less said about his conversion of *Moore's Melodies* to Irish the better. He died in 1881. Illustrative of the dilemma in which the bishops of the last century found themselves is the fact that Dr MacHale did *not* support the Land League.

CHAPTER XII

'GOD SAVE IRELAND!'

THE six years, which I spent in the College, went by and they were all the same, almost. There was no difference between them but in the stages of the work we had to do. Each year had its own stage of work allotted to it—one year advocacy, one year of arts, and, then, four years of theology. I put these behind me, without anything unusual happening. I got no more prizes. I made no effort to get them. I had a different kind of care! From the first year on, my health was threatening me and the threat was becoming more acute with each year, so that, by the time the end of the period was in sight, I didn't care about anything as long as I could walk out of the place. God granted me that (praise and thanksgiving be to Him). I received the orders, each one as I was entitled to it, until I was ordained a priest on the eleventh day of June, the summer of the year of the Lord's age, a thousand eight hundred, three score and seven.

I came home, but I was there only a few days when a letter came from the Bishop, telling me to go and take up duty in the parish of Kilshannig, beside Mallow. It is a great, long, wide parish, which stretches from Nadanuller east to the edge of Ballynamona and from the banks of the Blackwater southwards to Ahadallane and to Barrahaurin almost. In the south side of the parish, on Been, I was sent to live. 'Beennamweel' is its full name: they used to call a hare *'míol mhaighe'* and, from the fact that there were a lot of hares in the place, the mountain was called 'Beann na Míol', 'The Peak of the Hares'. That's how the people of the place explained the name to me and I suppose they know best.

*　　*　　*

I must mention, before I move any farther away from my College days, something else which happened while I was there. So that this will be correctly understood, I must go back a while. When I was going to school in Carriganimmy, there was a boy at the same school by the name of Murty Moynihan. He was a young man almost, that time. He had a good head, power of reflection and ambition. He went south to Skibbereen, I think, to teach school, after he had left Carriganimmy.

I didn't hear further account of him until I was at school in Kanturk, learning Latin. Then we heard rumours from Skibbereen and from the countryside round about, that a band had been founded there and that they were set on an insurrection to break the power of England in Ireland and to free the Gaeil from the tyranny of the Saxons. The band were called 'Phoenixmen'. I don't think the government of Ireland took much notice of them. At last, a horrible rumour about them reached us. We were told that one of their own had turned traitor on the others; that he went and sold them; that he gave their names to the enemy, that they were arrested and were inside in prison, shackled in black manacles. I recall that I saw the name of Murty Moynihan among those of the men who were put inside. The man who had betrayed them, was an O'Sullivan; he used to be called 'Ó Súilliobháin Gallda' or 'Britain's O'Sullivan'. The old, old story as always!

> Oh for a tongue to curse the slave,
> Whose treason like a withering blight
> Comes o'er the counsels of the brave
> To blast them in their hour of might!

I think that the poetry would have been better, if this were said:

> 'Oh for a rope to hang the slave', etc.

But it matters not. Neither curse nor rope ever stopped the informer in Ireland. It was not possible as long as injustice was so heavy and injurious that honest people could not bear it without some secret endeavour against it—and, then, the crew behind the injustice always had money in plenty to give the liberal bribe to the informer. It was a woeful state of affairs! 'Rocks bound and dogs loose!' Injustice in the shape of right. The lie in the shape of truth. The iron heel in the shape of law. Injustice sitting up boldly on the bench of equity and, from there, convicting integrity. As long as I have a memory in my head, that is how things have been in Ireland. But now [in 1913], we can expect a change at last. The sign is on it: injustice is foaming with rage, she is afraid that she will be expelled from the bench! I trust that what she fears will be her fate.

The law wasn't brought to bear too severely on the Phoenixmen. The business was looked upon as something trivial. It was thought that it would be better not to make too much of it. The whole business quietened down—as far as could be seen, at any rate. There was a man, whose name was Jeremiah O'Donovan Rossa, mixed up in it; that name has cropped up again and again since then.[1]

I wasn't long in the college before more rumours began to reach us inside of another underground movement against England throughout the country. The name *'Fíní'* was given to the band who were thus employed; it came from the ancient term *'Fianna Éireann'*.[2] It seems that they were first called *'Fianna'*, that this was then anglicised to 'Fenians' and that was put back into Gaelic again as *'Fíní'*. They reckoned that they could protect themselves against the informer by giving no information to anyone other than that which could not be sold—being of no use to the enemy, it would not be bought from anyone. However, all that did was to leave in the keeping of certain leaders the useful information which, if they wished to sell it, would be highly paid for. Then, if there were twenty persons who would not sell, perhaps there might be one who would—and the evil of the matter is that there was a traitor. It could not have been otherwise.

I hear people, at times, coming down heavily on the people of Ireland, saying that 'if an Irishman was put on a spit over a fire, another Irishman could be found to turn it'. It's true, perhaps. But more than that is true. If an Englishman was put on a spit over a fire, an Englishman could be found to turn it. If a Spaniard, or German, or Frenchman, or a man of any other nation in the world, was put on the spit, a person of the same nation—or two, or three, or four of them—could be found to turn it. For more than a hundred years, there has been great glorying in the manner in which the people of America fought against England and defeated her, and threw off the yoke of England. Let anybody read an account of that war and he will see clearly that the Irish traitor is not worthwhile mentioning alongside the traitors who were around Washington late and early, playing the toady to him with their loyalty, *mar dheadh,* while, at the same time, there were big bribes in their pockets to hand him over, dead or alive, to the power of England. If you could make a comparison between the countries, it is my strong opinion that more loyal people would be found among the Gaeil—and less scoundrels—than among other nations. That does not afford much satisfaction to the mind, however, when one scoundrel—especially when he is trusted and has knowledge of basic things—is able to hang hundreds and annihilate their labours.

When the Phoenixmen saw what the informer had done on them, they decided to play the game from that on in such a way that no other Ó Súilliobháin Gallda could inform on them. They changed their name to that of 'Fenians'. They went back to the time of Fionn mac Cumhail to get the name. They thought, and it was true for them, that, as long as their sway endured in Ireland, Fionn and the Fianna Éireann protected this country from every foreign enemy. In our own time, it was not unsuitable to give the name 'Fenians' to a band who were set on banishing the foreign enemy from Ireland.

I had spent a couple of years inside in Maynooth before people were to be heard mentioning the Fenians. The people began to pass on the word that there was such a band; that they used to be out at nights in lonely places, learning how to handle firearms and swords. For the most part, they were a secret band, although not completely so. They had a newspaper in Dublin and those who were running it were not innocuous nor were they uninfluential. Jeremiah O'Donovan Rossa was the editor; he was a strong, bold, fearless man.

But the newspapermen did something that they had no right to do. The clergy of Ireland and the old people had a long acquaintance with attempts made to rebel against the power of England. They saw what was the end to the attempt made by O'Brien. They saw what was the end to the Whiteboy business. They saw the treachery and the hanging which Malachy Duggan did.[3] It was fast in their minds that the end to the Fenian business would be the same—young men sailing on an unhappy course for a time and, then, treachery, false testimony, blood money, hanging and transportation for these young Irish men—and *The Times,* England's guardian devil, slandering them viciously and praying that their going would be one of no return. The clergy and the priests understood this only too well and it was no wonder that they were trying to counsel the boys, to put them on the right course and keep them out of the Fenian bands. The heads of these bands were well aware of this side of the story.

'What,' they said to each other, 'is the good of us trying to get the young men together properly against England, while the priests have such a tight hold on them. It is necessary for us to set about loosening that hold.'

They set about it. Their paper made a tirade against any priest who had the courage to say to the boys of his parish to stay away from the Fenians or they'd regret it, that it was the gallows tree they'd get shortly, or transportation. That paper was continually getting home to the boys that the priests were taking part with the

English. That was a disgusting lie.⁴ A lot of things helped to further
this lie: the boys were very young; they had no recollection of the
old days, the days of the Whiteboys, of Malachy, of the hanging of
the McCarthy brothers. On the other hand, they knew well how
their own life was being spent, how every single one of them was
working hard each and every day in the week, and how every bit of
the profits of that work was going in rent. And now, according to
this paper, here were the priests assisting such injustice. It was
driven home to them that the priest was an enemy, an enemy of
Ireland and a friend of Ireland's enemies.

When I'd see such work in the paper, I would be mad with anger.
I knew only too well that the English used the iron heel in Ireland.
Because of it, I had a savage hatred against the English. I can not
recall a time when that hate was not lighting in my heart. I recall
that, when I was very small, somebody showed me a piece that was
in *The Times* saying that English laws were not severe enough on the
criminals—the Irish people. I recall that I took hold of the paper,
put it down on the ground and danced on it until it was in ribbons.
And here, now, was an Irish paper telling the world that I was a
friend of the same England and an enemy of Ireland!

But there was worse than that itself. The lie affected a lot of the
boys—for a while, at any rate. I used to come home from college
every summer, as I have said already. Before, when the boys would
meet me out in the country or on the Macroom road, they used to
be very friendly to me and respectful to the man they thought had
the makings of a priest in him. I noticed a change in the two last
summers, a disgusting change, a change that caused me bitterness,
dejection and affliction. Four or five boys used to meet me on the
Macroom road, and they marching fiercely, *'A gcosa acu 'á tharac in
aoinfheacht'* as is said in the *'Táin Bó Cuailgne'*. When they'd be going
by me, their faces would cloud over and darken and they'd look at
me out of the corner of their eyes, as a person would look at a
blackguard of a scoundrel.

*   *   *

Two years went by. The last spring that I spent in Maynooth
came. During the three seasons prior to St Patricks Day of that
spring, every kind of rumour about the Fenians was going about.
The insurrection was to be on All-Hallows Day. Then it was to
come on New Year's Day. Then it was to come without any doubt
on St Bridget's Day. At last, it came. Ten thousand men went out

from the city of Cork. Fine, young, strong men they were. If they had had the arms and the preparation and proper leadership, they would have done work that would have taken some of the arrogance from *The Times*. As it was, they set every landlord and shoneen in Ireland shivering in their boots, from Donaghadee to Cape Clear. But there was one thing that had to do with that insurrection which delighted me. All those boys, in their hundreds and thousands, were on their knees before a priest, where they were able to get priests, making their confessions so that they would be ready to go into the presence of God if they fell in the battle they thought was coming. That brought home to me that there was nothing in that bad look they used to give me, a year or two before, but the injustice a person may do to his own mind and heart, and to his own conscience, when bad counsel and bad company put him up to do something that is bluntly against his intelligence and heart.

We were all inside in the college the morning the insurrection began. Every kind of rumour was coming to us. 'Trains full of red-coats going south! Every train a half-mile in length! More trains, full of wounded soldiers, coming from the south! Streams of blood on the railroads from the wounded soldiers! The Curragh and all the barracks on it in the hands of the Fenians!' And so on.

The snow came. We were all weighing the *pros* and *cons* as to how we'd get home to the south, or would we have to walk it.

The snow continued. Then came a change in the news. There came the law; the prisoners; the court; the trials; and—the old, old story—the informer. One of the leaders. A man who had the knowledge and information of their entire affairs. A man who had been giving all that knowledge to their enemies, the Castle crew in Dublin, for a long time before that, without anyone knowing. A man of whom every one of the Fenians thought there did not live a more loyal person than he. And there he used to be among them, stuck into every counsel with them, each one more secret and more discreet than the others; he had all their names sent down to Dublin and the price of their blood promised to him, even at that time, having the full of his pockets of blood money. They would sooner have taken his advice than that of a priest—until they saw him there in the court, answering questions, and every word that was coming out of his mouth was squeezing the hemp-rope tighter round their necks. It was a woeful sight!

The law and the informer put an end to the insurrection. It wasn't long until the ten thousand men, who had gone out from the city of Cork saw that there was no use in their work; that the heads, who were to lead the entire work, were fast in prison chains. Then, what was there to do but for everyone to go into hiding until he could go overseas, unknown to the crowds of watchmen that the English had on the harbours.

We all came home from the college in the summer, and we hadn't got to walk it. I was, as I have said, to do my priestly duties in the parish of Kilshannig.

*   *   *

The following year (1868), I was in Kanturk at a meeting of the ecclesiastical chapter, myself and the other priests who belonged to the place, when we got the news that the 'Manchester Martyrs' had been hanged. We were all amazed and angry. We all realised that it had been by accident the policeman had been killed in the rescue of the Fenian prisoners in Manchester; no one was culpable of his death. We realised as well that the English people were going out of their minds with fear of the Fenians and that they were mad with anger to have it to say that the Fenians were able to throw them into such terror. It was because of the hatred the English people had for the Fenians and for the people of Ireland that these three men were hanged. They would never have been hanged if it hadn't been for the terror and fear and hatred in English hearts.

When the three were standing on the gallows' trapdoor with the rope round each man's neck, they kissed each other and, just before the floor was taken from under their feet, they cried, 'God save Ireland!' That saying has prevailed in Irish mouths since then and will do so as long as there is one person of Gaelic stock alive in the land of Éire. And all that time the fame of the three will grow in magnitude and in acclamation, while England's baseness will wax in odium.

NOTES TO CHAPTER XII

1. The name was to 'crop up' again with far-reaching repercussions within two years, when Patrick Pearse, later to become commander-in-chief of the republican forces during Easter Week, gave his famous oration over the grave of the Fenian patriot.

Jeremiah O'Donovan Rossa (Diarmuid Ó Donnabhain Rosa) was a

native-speaker from Rossmore (whence he took the name 'Rosa', i.e. 'of Ross') near the coast of west Cork. When James Stephens, known as 'the wandering hawk', the founder of Fenianism, visited Skibbereen in 1858, O'Donovan was head of the local Phoenix National and Literary Society. Gaoled in 1858 for treasonable activities and released two years later, he undertook an almost country-wide campaign as a Fenian organiser. In 1863, he became manager of the Fenian paper, the *Irish People,* in Dublin. Two years later, he was again charged with treason. The judge in his trial was the traitor Keogh; and O'Donovan, carrying out his own defence, attacked him savagely; as a result, his sentence was penal servitude for life! While in prison, he was elected M.P. for Tipperary (1869) and agitation for the release of the Fenians was begun. After eight years' penal servitude, O'Donovan Rossa was released on condition that he left the United Kingdom for ever. In fact, he returned over thirty years later to unveil the monument to the Fenians in Skibbereen! He played an important role in American Fenianism and became something of a god to the entire movement. There was an almost mythical quality about everything he did, whether it was throwing a bucket of water into the face of the governor of Millbank prison or interrupting the House of Commons in London with a political speech. As Pearse said in his oration when the dead Fenian was brought back to Ireland in 1915, O'Donovan Rossa typified Fenianism.

2. Literally 'soldiers of Ireland'. The especial term refers to the warriors of the legendary Fionn Mac Cumhail ('Finn McCool the Giant' of the travel-brochures), main figure of the Fiannaíocht or Ossianic tales and poetry.

3. Note the rebellions which come automatically into O'Leary's mind: Smith O'Brien's 'cabbage-patch' rebellion of 1848 (see *The Great Hunger*), the Whiteboys and other 'agrarian outrages'. These and the Tithe War are still almost unchronicled and, even yet, paid scant attention by our historians. To those like O'Leary who were in the mainstream of tradition, the Gaeil had been in a continuous state of rebellion—a view held by the British government. Fenianism, because of its roots, had an enormous attraction for the people; so deep-rooted was it that neither Socialist nor French Revolutionary theories ever penetrated to its core.

4. Although Canon O'Leary's sincere consideration for his flock, his 'people of Ireland', is never in doubt, one cannot help suspecting his naïveté here. The part played by the leaders of the Roman Catholic Church in the Fenian era, up to and including the post-Parnellite fracas, is of immense historical interest and controversy. See Appendix 12.

CHAPTER XIII

IN KILSHANNIG AND KILWORTH

WHILE I was in Kilshannig parish, I had to say two Masses every Sunday and holiday; I used give a sermon in English at one of them and in Gaelic at the other. There are three chapels in the parish, one apiece in Kilfether, Glantane and Beennamweel. It has to be called Beannamweel to distinguish it from another 'Been'—Beenalacht—to the south-west of it. It's often a call for oils came to me in the night from Beenalacht.

I remember a certain sick-call—there's no danger that I'd ever lose the memory of it! A boy ran into the house, panting so much that it was only with difficulty that he could talk.

'There's a man dying, Father,' says he.

'Where's this?' says I.

'West at Beenalacht, Father.'

'What's on him?'

'He swallowed his tongue, Father.'

'*Aililiú*!' I said. 'How could he swallow his tongue?'

'He was drinking thick milk, Father, and he swallowed his tongue along with the milk! He hasn't a word of speech,' says he, 'and when we looked into his mouth, we couldn't get any sight of his tongue. I'm afraid that you won't find him alive, Father.'

I headed off for the west. I found him alive: he could speak when I reached him.

'*Airiú*! What caused you to swallow your tongue?' says I to him.

'*O mhaise*!' he says, 'that fool of a boy! I had a thirst and I drank the drink too fast, and a cramp or some such thing came in my throat so that the tongue went into a lump back altogether into my gullet. That fella supposed that I had swallowed my tongue! He's no sense.'

The cramp was gone from the poor man's throat, anyway. He had no need of the oil and so I came home at my leisure.

It is not without reason that the townland is called Beenalacht, the Peak of the Standing Stones. The stones are there. First of all, there are two great, broad circles of them, one inside the other and both concentric. These are made of stones, placed in a standing position as if they were tombstones. Then, to the south-west of the outside circle, there are two lines of stones, each standing in a similar manner. The lines run side by side and are not too far apart; I don't recall now what this distance was, but I would imagine that it was four or five yards or thereabouts. There were a couple or three stones at the far end, joining the lines together to make up a parallelogram. It is more than four and forty years since I saw them.

There's a road west from Beennamweel to Nadanuller and to Kilcorney. Many years before I came to the area, there was a certain priest living in Kilcorney. He was struck down with an illness. He thought he would be himself again for the following Sunday, but he wasn't. There was a priest, with whom he was very friendly, over in Ballynamona. He sent off a messenger on Saturday afternoon to ask this priest to come, if it were possible, and to say Mass in his place in Kilcorney. The Ballynamona priest had a very good horse and the name he had on him was 'Gríosach'.[1] He rose early on the Sunday morning and off to the west with him, by Ahadallane, by Beennamweel, through Glannaharee and Nadanuller, into Kilcorney chapel. He said the Mass exactly at the appointed time, not one minute later. It seems that, perhaps, some of the congregation were used to the Mass being a little bit late—whatever it was, there was a lot of them late for Mass that same Sunday. The priest was going back to his own town, after saying the Mass, when he met up with some of the congregation on the road. They were coming to Mass and he with the Mass said already. He had to be back in time to say Mass the same morning in Ballynamona after he'd get home. He spoke to the people who were late.

'Oho!' said he, with a rann in Gaelic,

> 'Gríosach, that slept in Ballynamona,
> 'Twas he snatched the Mass from the folk of Kilcorney!'

Sick calls used to come to me all the way from the banks of Blackwater in the north, and often they'd come in the middle of the night. Sometimes, perhaps, I would have been down there during the day, doing Sunday duties or visiting the schools. Then, when I'd be sound asleep, in the middle of the night, the sick call would come and I'd have to rise and go off down again. But I was young and strong that time and I didn't take much heed of things of the sort.

At that time, everybody used to speak Gaelic to me when I'd go like that to put the oils on them. Although some of them were fairly young, the messengers themselves used to speak it to me.

The parish priest, who was over them there, had fine Gaelic.

Fr Thomas Murray was his name. He had come up from Carbery, before two dioceses were made of the diocese of Cloyne and Ross. He was upwards of three score years and ten when he and I were in the parish of Kilshannig and he lived until he was four score and eleven. When I had been a year and a season in the parish, the Bishop sent me eastwards to Kilworth, and, a little while after that, Fr Thomas went south to Iniscarra. It was there that he died, after being a priest for three score years. For some of that time, his work was severe. He saw all the bad times. He saw the people dying at the foot of the ditches and on the roads—when food was going overseas to make rent for the landlords. I cannot think of it now itself without a fit of rage coming over me.

I well recall the day I left Beennamweel to go east to Kilworth. The Bishop's letter had been delayed for some reason. It didn't reach me until the Saturday morning and I had to be in Kilworth the following Sunday to say two Masses, the first out in Araglin and the twelve o'clock in Kilworth.

I had a good mare and a nice, little trap. I went along into Mallow and took the road east from there. When I had gone a couple of miles, I observed that the day was darkening.

'I'm afraid we'll have thunder,' said I, in my own mind.

With that, there came a strong, heavy noise, the like of which I had never heard before.

'That isn't thunder,' I said to myself.

I halted the mare and stopped for a while to see would I hear it again. I didn't. I was thinking and thinking to find something to which I could liken it but I failed to remember any sort of noise I could put in comparison to it. It was very strong, very heavy. A person would imagine that it was in the sky and in the ground at the one time. If it had spoken a second time, I could have, perhaps, made a guess as to what kind of noise it was, but it didn't. I continued on my way and the noise went out of my head.

I found the road from Mallow to Kilworth longer by far than I had thought. It was making out on twelve in the night when I reached the place. After night had come down on me, I lost a good deal of time calling on people, who were asleep, to ask the way. I reached Kilworth. All the doors were closed and the people asleep. I saw a light in one house, and headed for that. I called out to the people of the house. A woman came to the door to me. I told her who I was and asked her if she could give me shelter until day, as I had to go out in the morning to Araglin to say Mass there.

'Ochón, Father,' she said, 'I will and welcome; and most certainly the accommodation I am able to give you is not too good. But let it be good or bad, it isn't too long we will have this house to give shelter to anyone. We ourselves are to be evicted on Monday morning. Come in, Father,' said she.

I went in. There was an empty house outside in the yard, in which I put the mare and gave her something to eat. I had that in the little trap. I was given sleeping accommodation as fine as the poor people were able to afford. I was up in the morning at the first light. The woman of the house gave me the directions and signs of the road, and I went on my way eastwards to the new chapel of Araglin. When the congregation had gathered, I said Mass for them, and then I headed south-westwards again for Kilworth, and I was there at twelve to say the second Mass.

On the following Monday morning, I was looking at the paper. Nothing interested me much until I laid eyes on this:

EXTRAORDINARY OCCURRENCE

About 2 o'clock p.m. on Saturday last a distinct shock of earthquake was felt in the neighbourhood of Mallow. It was accompanied by a loud subterranean noise which lasted only a moment. Several persons felt the shock and heard the sound.

I realised then what was the meaning of that noise I had heard a couple of miles east of Mallow the Saturday before. Some time in the autumn, in the year of the Lord eighteen sixty-eight, that noise was heard and that single earth tremor was felt. I didn't notice the tremor—probably because I was in the car and the car going.

While I was in Kilworth that time, I spent more than a year living in a house on a hillock overlooking Araglin bridge. I was told that Baron Piggott had lived in the same house, when he was young and a student. He was a judge in Dublin, when I lived in the house. Baile-idir-dhá-abhainn is the name given to the townland—'The townland between two rivers'. The Araglin river runs into the Blackwater to the east of the town, and the Funchion runs into the west, which leaves the townland between the two rivers. A while south of the house, there's an old castle, and the Rightheaghlach, or 'Royal Household', is the name of it; Rathealy is the name given to it in English, so that a person would suppose that this came from some one of the Healy people. That's how English ruins everything Gaelic with which it has any contact.

I wasn't living long on the hill at Baile-idir-dhá-abhainn, when I got to know all the roads throughout the parish. I was told that there was a holy well in the eastern corner of the parish, 'Tobar na hOla' it was called. As soon as I heard about it, I went east to see it. The place, where it is, is a very lonely one. A nice, little well it is, with very fine water. I took a drink of it and liked it well. I was told that people used to make visits to it, doing the 'round' of the well, and that, once in the year, there used be a pattern there. I was told that, at a certain pattern, when a great number of people were gathered there, a fierce fight arose among them, that blood was spilt, plenty of it, that then a curse was put on the place and it was known as 'Tober na Fola', 'The Well of Blood', instead of 'Tobar no h-Ola', 'The Well of the Unction'.

The main road from Cork to Dublin, the coach road as it is called, goes northwards through Kilworth and the middle of the hills. The hills are very desolate. Some time ago, they were even more desolate than they are now or even when I was in the parish. A highwayman used frequent that road, robbing the people. It happened that a poet by the name of Éamonn Wall was going along one day. He came to a place that was very lonely and the highwayman sprang out before him from the ditch of the road. Seamas Freeney was the robber's name. He raised his pistol before the poet.

'Hand me any money you have,' says he.

'I haven't a ha'penny of money, sonny,' said the poet. 'Come here and search me, if you suppose I have.'

Freeney looked at him. 'Whether you have money or not,' said he, 'there isn't much signs of it on you. But I see you have new boots, wherever you got them.' He looked down at the old broken shoes on his own feet. 'I imagine,' he said, 'that those new boots would suit me. Take them off you.'

He had to do so.

'Throw them over,' said Freeney.

He threw them.

'Draw back down there a piece from me now,' says Freeney.

He drew back. Then Freeney took off his own old boots and put the new ones on him. When they were on his feet, he stood up and tried them out to see how they suited him. 'Oh,' says he, 'they're lovely, lovely altogether. They suit me as well as if they were made for me. 'Here,' he said, throwing the old boots to the poet, 'let you have them ones.'

The poet put on the old boots and set off about his own business, and Freeney went over the hill.

Another poet heard the tale of the boots. He made this verse:

I'm sorry and sore for the fear you took, Éamonn,—
Like a cold-footed yokel with the knees of him caving—
We were holding the opinion that you'd stand against eighty,
But here you go and throw over your new boots to Freeney![2]

This verse was going from mouth to mouth. Éamonn heard it.
He gave this answer to it:

Your poetry, young poet, 'tis cutting you've made it!
It was no fear came o'er me to set my knees quaking,
But a rogue of the road with a bullet constrained me—
Who set store on my soul as worthless than a ha'penny![3]

They told me of another deed the same Freeney did. The coach
came by from Cork one day. There was a woman on it from Dublin
and she just had to be talking—her mouth never had a rest, but
kept on asking everybody else on the coach if they supposed there
was any danger that the highwayman would meet up with them.

'I've a thousand pounds here,' she would say, every now and
again, 'and what'll I do at all if he meets up with us?'

They put the road behind them without any trouble until they
left Kilworth to the south and they were making on the mountain.
When they were in the most desolate part of the mountain, out
comes Freeny. As soon as he spoke to the driver, the coach halted.
Freeney came to the door with his pistol levelled.

'Yes, dear friends, let's have no row, but hand out to me what
money ye have.'

There was a man there, who had hardly spoken since he left
Cork. Crying with the fright, he called out as soon as Freeney
spoke. 'Oh, sir,' he said, and he pulled out all the money in his
pocket—the full of his hand of small-money, 'that's all I have and
don't shoot me. Here it is for you and don't kill me. I don't know
has anyone else here got much, but look, that lady there has a
thousand pounds. Hand him that thousand pounds of yours,
madame, so that he won't shoot us!'

She was forced to give the thousand pounds to the robber.
Freeney was laughing and he had his reason for it. He didn't go too
hard on the others. He took whatever they gave him and went
away. It was then that the woman who lost the thousand pounds,
had the talk! Her mouth never rested from cursing and abusing the
man who had spilled the secret on her. He didn't speak any more.
They reached the city of Dublin. As soon as the coach stopped,
within the city, the quiet man put his hand into his pocket, pulled

out a piece of paper and handed it to the woman who had all the talk.

'Here,' he said. 'This is your thousand pounds.'

What was the piece of paper but an order on the Bank of Dublin for a thousand pounds!

'Look,' said he, 'I've ten thousand pounds here with me. I'm taking it from the Bank of Cork to the Bank of Dublin. It's in gold I have it. We were afraid to leave the gold in Cork for we got word that the bank was to be broken into. I was forced to take my chance with Freeney and bring the gold with me. If it hadn't been for you and your thousand pounds, my ten thousand was gone from me.'

When the woman saw the name that was down on the piece of paper, she was satisfied. She knew the man, whose name it was—it was the same man who had given her the piece of paper, but he was disguised so well, she hadn't recognised him at all. When he told her who he was, she was highly pleased.

I don't know if the story is true. I am only telling it as it was told to me.

I learned how Freeney was killed in the end. He met up with a gentleman, who was after getting a sum of money that day.

'Hand me the money you have there,' said Freeney to him.

'I suppose I have no way out of it,' the gentleman said, and he threw a heavy purse from him onto the ground. Freeney bent to lift the purse. While doing so, the gentleman snatched a pistol out of his own pocket and put a bullet through the bending man. That bullet wounded him, but it didn't kill him immediately. He straightened up and turned the mouth of his own pistol on the gentleman, who reckoned that the hour of his death had come. But Freeney halted without firing the shot.

'Your blood won't be on my hands,' he said. 'I'm going into the presence of God. That which I have against me already isn't small.'

He went off over the ditch. Some days afterwards, a while from the place, he was found dead.[4]

The people had a great affection for him. He used to divide among the poor people a good share of the money he took from the rich. Without a doubt, there was nothing in that prodigality but 'being free and easy with another's strip of leather'; yet, all the same, the people were grateful to him and they'd give him shelter whenever he'd have need of it.

It wasn't only with the poor people that he used to be liberal at times. A gentleman met with him one night.

'Hand me whatever money you have,' says Freeney.

The gentleman handed him a great purse of money. 'Look now, Seamas,' said he. 'It's my opinion that you wouldn't do that much on me, if you rightly understood how things are with me.'

'What is it that I don't understand?' said Seamas.

'That money isn't mine at all,' the gentleman said. 'That's rent I got today from such-and-such a landlord's tenants, and I have to give it to the landlord, no matter what place I procure it. Himself won't be put out one ha'penny by this business.'

'Is that the way it is?' Seamas said.

'It is surely,' said the other man.

'Right-o,' Seamas said. 'I won't put that hardship on you. If I were able to take the money from himself, I'd be satisfied to do it—but it's not from you that I can rightly take his piece. Here's your purse. But let yourself give me a couple of pounds on loan. I've a use for it.'

He gave it. And it's many a night's lodgings and good meal of food Seamas got in that gentleman's house afterwards, when he was badly in need of them.

* * *

Araglin Church was newly built. It was very high, and the wind, when it rises at all, belabours the little hill on which it is built. I could not help thinking it was a great pity the church wasn't placed down on the secluded land beside the river rather than on the crown of the little hill. When I was living on that hill over Araglin bridge, I had to come down to Kilworth to say Mass and make sick-calls. Often, it was in the middle of the night the sick-calls would come. I knew that if I had been living in the village I would have been close to my work, day and night. In the end, there was a change. A doctor, who had been living in the village, decided to move north to Mitchelstown. As soon as he was gone from Kilworth I took the house and came down to live there. I was now where my work was. In addition to that, I was in the centre of the parish. Although I still had long roads to travel, most of them were twice the journey when I used live at Araglin bridge.

There's a townland away over in the north-eastern side of the parish, by the name of Gortnaskehy, which is nine miles from Kilworth. It's often a call for oils came to me in the middle of the night from that townland. I used to be awake at times and I'd hear the messenger coming on horseback, at a trot, and 'Gort-na-Sceiche! Gort-na-Scheice!' the trotting feet of the horse on the road would say and I awake in the bed listening, 'Gort-na-Sceiche! Gort-na-Scheice!', and I thinking on the nine miles of a way that was before me. It wouldn't put me out much, however. As soon as I'd be in the saddle, I wouldn't have preferred to be in my bed. I was young that time.[5]

NOTES TO CHAPTER XIII

1. 'Burning Embers'.
2. Is brón liom an sgeon so do ghlacais, a Éamoinn,
    Mar chóbach neamhchródha gan neart 'n-a ghéagaibh:
    'S gurt dóich linn, dar ndóchaint, gur cheap le céad tu!
    'S do bhróga do sheoladh 'n-a ghlaic chun Freíní!
3. A óigfhir nach feollta do chanas bhérsa,
    Ní dreoileacht neamhchródha do bhain dom féinig:
    Ach rógaire ar bhóthar do ghread le pléir mé,
    'S nár mhó aige siúd feoirling ná anam Éamoinn!
4. History records a Captain Freeney (d. 1789), a notorious highwayman, who betrayed his gang for a pardon; but there is some evidence of an earlier Freeney operating in the Kilworth mountains.
5. Canon Sheehan's novels, *My New Curate* and *The Blindness of Doctor Grey*, portray the country priests as being for the most part men of large physique and iron constitution who might spend ten hours a day on horseback, either succouring or chastising their flocks; their words, he wrote, cut like razors and hands smote like lightning. Below are translations of two contemporaneous *búrdún* to add to the picture:

    A penny from the living, two from the dead,
    a pound marrying and a crown baptising,
    horses without coaches on long roads,
    gave many a priest a life without ease.

And

    I'd like a priest to be fine, cheerful, merry,
    full of faith and charity, good-natured,
    who'd be kind to the poor and gentle with his flock;
    but I'd not like a boor in the fair livery of the Only-Son.

CHAPTER XIV

PROMOTING TOTAL ABSTINENCE

I WASN'T long out of the college—a priest at last and doing the work of a priest among the people—when I took note of one thing in particular: the terrible damage drink was doing to the Irish people. I saw the tradesman stuck in the public house every Saturday evening, staying there until his week's pay, or the most of it, would be gone, while his wife and children were at home without supper, perhaps without any clothes in reasonable condition; and then, on the Sunday morning, that man unable to rise or go off to Mass. I saw the wife and the wits taken from her from trying to take care of the man and his family and house without the necessary money— herself half-naked and the hearth cold and empty, without fire or the makings of a fire, without heat or comfort. I saw the farmer coming home drunk from the fair or market, himself and his horse in danger of falling into the ditch of the road, there to be drowned or crushed; and the money, which he had a right to bring home, left behind him in the public-houses at every cross- roads he came to—and a liberal profit given into every house of them. Throwing away a bright half-crown in each place didn't mean any more to him than a spit of tobacco! And then, when his senses would come to him the morning after that, a person would imagine that a red ha'penny was worth a half-sovereign from the way he'd be giving some little amount to his wife to provide things for the house!

I saw all these evils, and a thousand others along with them. It was drummed into my mind that it would be right for me to make some effort to counteract them, whether that be in a small way or large; if it was a thing that I could only succeed in doing a little itself, that would be better than not doing anything at all.

To ask every one to abstain from alcoholic drink—I realized that that was the only way to set about the business. I knew well that it would be hard to get many people to make that pledge. I knew, also, that I would have to have a very bold front if I asked any person to take the pledge without myself doing it along with the others. It was I had to make the beginning. I did it, too. I made up my mind in the presence of God not to take alcoholic drink any more. Then I began to counsel the people to do likewise.

Although some of the old people and some of those who were in middle-age failed me, the young people did not. I wasn't long living in the village of Kilworth, when I noticed the small gorsoons running wild all over the place every evening. I thought that it would be a good thing to get a small room with nice books for them and to gather them together, reading the books, for an hour or a couple of hours of the clock, every evening. There was no book in Gaelic to be had in any place at that time—unless a person procured the Foreign Bible, but you couldn't have anything to do with that because of the bad name the *Soupers* had left it.[1]

I wrote to Dublin and I got books that were as Gaelic as books in English could be: *The Story of Ireland, Poets and Poetry of Munster, Speeches from the Dock* and so forth. Baron Piggott[2] was alive in Dublin at the time. He heard the story of the boys and their books and he sent ten pounds to us to buy more books. We did so—good, basic English books, such as Shakespeare and Milton and their likes. We had a good library of books the boys had never heard any mention of until then. They'd come in early every single night, when we'd have the long evenings, and they'd be reading the books, every boy with his own, until it was time for stopping. Then, I myself would read to them—a little bit from the life of a saint—and I'd send them home. I recall that I gave many nights over to reading the *Life of the Curé d'Ars* to them and that they took a great interest in it.

After a time, I persuaded them to abstain from every alcoholic drink, and they did it eagerly. I made up little cards for them and got the promise printed on the card, like this:

> Towards satisfaction for my sins and towards avoiding every sin from this on, with the help of God and in honour of St Brigid, I will abstain from every alcoholic drink.

We put the entire business, ourselves and the library, under the protection of St Brigid. I had word later on that many of the boys kept up that promise for a long time and that some of them kept it up for the duration of their lives.

When St Brigid's Day would come, we'd have a small feast with sweets and cakes and other dainties of the sort. We had a very special drink and in that we would drink the toast to our saint, to Brigid, 'The Mary of the Gaeil' as she was called long ago. There is a fine spring-water well down in Baile-idir-dhá-abhainn, called the 'Well of the Fort'. We'd send down a horse and car, with a fine, big churn in the car, to the well and get the full of the churn of water brought back to us; and it'd be in a glass of that water every one of us would drink the toast to our saint.

We had another card and these were the thoughts that were on it:

I love God!
I love the Faith!
I love Ireland!

I hate pride!
I hate ignorance!
I hate discord!

I will not boast!
I will not quarrel!
I will not get drunk!

That was a white card; the other was a green one. Every one of our band had these two cards. They took them home with them. I won't say that the odd card is not to be found in some of the houses throughout the parish still.

The words that were on the cards were in English. It wasn't possible to get the words in Gaelic printed on them at the time. There was far more Gaelic being spoken in the parish at the time than English. In addition to that, the Gaelic there was excellent. I used to think it grand to be listening to the old people speaking. When I would put the Last Unction on one of them and give him the Holy Body, and when he would say, from his heart out, 'My Lord Jesus Christ is my love! He is my love for ever!', my breath would stop on me and a quickening of the heart would come on me with tears springing from my eyes, so that I would have to turn aside a little.

That was the speech that had the faith in it! That was the kind of holy people who were in Ireland at the time and before it, and they without a word of English. It was a vain business for the enemy to be trying to compel the likes of these to deny the faith.

There were four 'National' schools in the parish and not one of the teachers teaching in them had as much as one single word of Gaelic. That was a terrible injustice to both teachers and young folk alike. The teachers were killing themselves trying to teach through a language that was not understood, and the minds of those who were learning were being tormented, blinded and sent astray from trying to take in knowledge through the unknown tongue. And then—another injustice more disastrous on top of these!—an inspector would come from the Board and, going into these schools, would test and examine—and he quite blind to the two wrongs.

I have to say this much, however. As far as the work went in the schools (the amount of it that could be done in spite of all the wrongs), it was done in a manner that amazed me. The knowledge was given to the young people and they absorbed it—through the hard road of English, through the foreign road of English—in a way that would have done credit to both teachers and learners had it been otherwise. It was intellectual ability on all sides which accounted for such a good result from the work.

But the people, who were in middle age that time (those who were neither old nor at school), were speaking English and I don't suppose that there ever was a more horrible language spoken from the mouths of people than that same English. Note well the labour that this caused both teachers and children: that horrible English was normally spoken to the children at home, while the teachers were trying to teach some kind of more presentable English to them in the school. And then the inspector would come and he'd trample on everything: reviling the teachers (often before the children) when they failed to get correct English into the children's mouths, and reviling the children when one of them would say 'I do be' or 'We does be'.

I was listening once to an inspector. He put a question to a child about what had kept him at home the day before, or something of the sort.

'I does be thinning turnops, sir,' the child said.

'And what does your brother be doing?' the inspector said.

'He do be minding the cows, sir?' said the child.

' "I does be", "He do be". That is nice teaching!' he said to the teacher.

'Well, Mr "Do be",' he said to the child, 'how are you today, Mr "Do be"? And how is old Mr "Do be"? And how is Mrs "Do be"? And how are all the other little "Do be's" and "Does be's"?'

Here he was referring to the child's father and mother and the rest of the family at home. Note that for an insult to the household! A public insult, before the entire school!

Let nobody think that this sort of thing happened but seldom. It used to happen often, very often. At times, it happens still. I often saw an inspector striding into a school, with his hat on his head, and having nothing for the teacher, in front of the children, but the most insulting words in his jowels.

I spent four years in Kilworth. The library was quite large at the end of the period. The great war between France and Germany came about in the course of that time. During the years of the war, we'd have the papers in the library to read about the way it was going and, without a doubt, the sympathies of all, both young and old of us, were with France. We were very sorry when we saw Germany with the victory.

During that time also, our Irish parliamentarians, with Isaac Butt as their leader, were 'standing for their rights' over in the English Parliament.[3] We used to have great meetings in every part of Ireland to make common cause with Butt and his band in that work. I recall that a big party of the people of Kilworth went to Mitchelstown one Sunday to a big meeting which was held there. I had to go with them. We thought we'd done great work when we had that day over us. We had almost freed Ireland from the tyranny of the Foreigners, according to us!

NOTES TO CHAPTER XIV

1. By the 'Foreign Bible', the author, of course, was referring to the Protestant Bible; the soupers were the hated Protestant proselytizers who, in the 'bad times', gave soup in exchange for professions of faith.
2. David Richard Piggott, born in Kilworth, 1797. Appointed King's Counsel in 1835, he was elected M.P. for Clonmel in 1839. He had a reputation for literary attainments and, as his generosity to the Kilworth group indicates, was typical of a new species among the gentry. His eldest son, John Edward, was a Young Irelander of note and contributor to the Nation; of more importance, perhaps, was his splendid work in the field of Irish music.
3. This was the Home Rule League, founded in 1870 by Isaac Butt, one of Ireland's almost-forgotten patriots. A Donegal-born Protestant and at first a Unionist, he had been one of Daniel O'Connell's most influential opponents. Butt, who was to become the most able barrister in the country, gradually became something of a Nationalist. It was not the horrors of the Great Famine alone which caused him to urge radical reform of land tenure—a position which automatically led him to seek for a native parliament. He was Liberal-Conservative M.P. for Youghal from 1852 to 1862. For four years, Butt acted as chief defending counsel for many of the Fenian leaders and, as he had earlier done when defending the Young Irelanders, won the admiration of the Nationalists. He was, in turn, deeply impressed by the integrity of the felons and began to work for Home Rule. The aims of the League were moderate: to win for Ireland the right to manage her own internal affairs. It's first members were well-to-do Protestants but the main support was later to come from the Catholic middle-classes and many of the clergy. The memory of Butt and his League has been overshadowed by that of Parnell's Irish Party, into which it developed.

CHAPTER XV

OUR SCHOOL IN RATHCORMACK

WHEN the time came as the Bishop thought fit, I was sent south-wards over the Blackwater, to Rathcormack. I wasn't long in this parish until I began the same work as I had going on in Kilworth. I gathered some of the boys of the village and spoke to them. I told them of what had been going on in Kilworth, about the books and the two cards and, especially, about the abstinence from drink. The cards were accepted and the abstinence promised. We took a house over, books were bought, we had our library under the patronage of St Brigid—just as was in Kilworth.

It wasn't long until I realised that a lot of the Rathcormack boys knew something about music. We used to have singing. These were songs in English, however, as there wasn't one word of Irish spoken in the little village. But, if they were in English itself, they were lovely, so good were the voices and so sweet the strains, with volume full and hearts high.

Some of the boys, besides, had a good knowledge of musical instruments—of flutes and fiddles. I came up with the idea that, perhaps, it might be a good thing, since they had a fondness for music and had such ability, to provide them with brass instruments and we'd have a band. We got forty pounds together and sent for some of the brass instruments. I spoke to one of the army musicians in Fermoy and I asked him to come out to us at Rathcormack a couple of times a week and to teach the boys how to handle and get the music from the instruments. We agreed on the payment he'd get and so he came to us. He was doing so for a time—it wasn't too long. Some of the boys picked up the knowl-edge quickly, so that they were able to teach the others. We were then able to go ahead on our own and didn't have to be paying our money to the man in the red-coat. Before much time had gone by, the boys were able to handle the instruments like experts, skilfully and dexterously, and they'd play music as well as any army band would.[1]

I had been in Rathcormack about two years, when that much had been achieved. It was then exactly that a letter came to me from Dublin, telling me that a group had been founded in the city 'to keep Gaelic alive'.[2]

'By the deer,' said I to myself, 'if it's a good thing, it's high time for it!'

I forwarded them a letter, asking them to send me the booklets they had. I told the boys what I had done. They used often hear me giving a sermon in Gaelic to the Sunday congregation. They all said immediately that they would like to learn Gaelic. I put a copy of the booklet into the hand of each boy and they started to learn the words. There were very simple, little words in the first lessons—like this, as far as I can recall now:

lá	=	a day	breagh	=	fine
bó	=	a cow	bán	=	white
gé	=	a goose	dubh	=	black
cat	=	a cat	mór	=	big
bean	=	a woman	beag	=	little

Then, there was another lesson like this:

lá breagh	=	a fine day	bean beag	=	a little woman
bó mór	=	a big cow	bean mór	=	a big woman
gé bán	=	a white goose	bó maith	=	a good cow
cat dubh	=	a black cat	bó dubh	=	a black cow

We got past a few of the lessons. Then, when the boys had learned that much, we were told this piece of information:

The true Irish for a 'big cow' is really not 'bó mór', but 'bó mhór'. So also with those other instances; the true Irish is not 'bean mór', but 'bean mhór'; not 'bean beag' but 'bean bheag'; not 'bó maith' but 'bo mhaith"; not 'bó dubh' but 'bó dhubh'. We really considered it better not to burthen the learner at the beginning with the mysteries of Irish aspiration (or some such thing).[3]

As soon as the boys saw that much, they said, 'What is this! We were first taught to say 'bó dubh', and now we are told that 'bó dubh" is wrong, and that we must say "bó dhubh"! Why were we not told the right word from the start?'

They went on strike. They would not learn any more Gaelic out of those books. I went on strike as well as them. I realised that it was no good depending on any group who thought they could keep Gaelic alive with this kind of business. Whenever any of the old speakers would hear 'bó mór' and 'bó dubh' and 'bean beag', they used to be putting their souls out laughing.[4]

I noticed that some of the boys had intelligence, light of reason and reflective power above the ordinary—a few of them far above

the ordinary. It struck me forcibly that it would be a great pity not
to give them an opportunity to make some beneficial use of these
qualities.

My own knowledge of the ancient langauges, of Latin and Greek,
had been getting more dull, more inaccurate and more clouded.
'By the deer!' I said to myself, 'perhaps I couldn't do a better thing
than to gather my old Latin and Greek books to me and to set
about teaching those noble and ancient tongues to one or two of
the boys. Who knows what result might come from it later on?
Whether or not a good result might arise afterwards, there was one
would come out of it in the present: I would renew my own
knowledge and that'd be no harm to me.'

I drew the old books to me, wiped the dust from them and began
to look through them; it was short before I saw that there was a
need for a renewal. I spoke to one of the boys, the best man of
them; Thomas Moore was his name. He was the best at music, at
book-reading and every other kind of mental work we had going
on. I asked him if he would like to learn Latin.

'What business would I have for it, Father?' he said.

'Who knows, but God might might make a priest of you,' I said.
'If you'd like to learn Latin, I will teach it to you, and you won't
have to pay but the one thing for the work.'

'And what is that, Father?' said he.

'This much, Thomas. If God opens the road for you to become a
priest, that you will continue to abstain from drinking and that you
will do your best to see that others will do the same.'

'I'll do that, Father,' he said. 'And, certainly, if it be God's will
for me, I'd give the whole world to be a priest.'

'That's grand,' said I. 'Here's the book, look, and here's the first
lesson you have to learn. It's as well for us to begin now.'

And we began. It wasn't long until we had the second boy
working along with us. Before we had put three weeks by us, there
were seven learning Latin from me. I assure you that I was forced
to look to myself and to polish up my portion of the old
knowledge and to regulate and arrange it. It's amazing what good
hands for asking questions boys between twelve and fifteen are! I
got a better knowledge of Latin during that renewal and teaching
than I got when I used to be learning it in Macroom or Kanturk
or Maynooth College itself. Teaching teaches far better than
learning does!

There was a boy living to the north, beside Mitchelstown, whose
name was Terence Shealy. He had a relation, a very respectable

woman, living near Rathcormack and she knew that Terence's great aim was to be a priest. She told him about the work I was doing. Down he comes to me from the north. He began learning Latin. I suppose he was about twelve or thirteen but I soon noticed that he had the reasoning power, the flair and the spirit of learning.

Here was a school, then—with music and reading of books, and everything going ahead beautifully. Neither myself nor the boys were tied to the work. When parish work took me away, the boys would go home for themselves and would do the work there as best they could—and thought up questions to put to me when I'd come back again to them!

We had a great time of it altogether, myself and themselves, me teaching and they learning from me and joy of mind on all of us. I don't suppose that there's another joy to be had in this life which is gladder than that joy of mind which visits a teacher and his learners when they are of one accord in their work, when they understand each other, when their only object, foundation and aim is honour to God and benefit for the faith. We had that joy then and the work went ahead with us, gloriously.

NOTES TO CHAPTER XV

1. Once when talking to an old musician, I asked him why the playing of the uillinn-pipes, once so popular, had been in danger of dying out in the latter half of the last century. 'Weren't they blared off the face of the earth by the temperance brass bands!' was the retort. In this age of television, it is easy to forget the important position local bands have held in the past—even up to 25 years ago. I can recall, from the neighbourhood of the north-western village where I was reared, three bands—brass, fife-and-drum, bagpipes—being marshalled for every notable event from elections to feiseanna. Their demise came all too fast; by the mid-1950s, not one existed.

2. The Society for the Preservation of the Irish Language. See Appendix 13.

3. It is hard to credit it but some teachers still 'really consider it better not to burthen the learner with the mysteries of Irish aspiration'! There is no mystery, of course, once the learner (and teacher) realises that the use of the tongue is all-important while the use of the lower-jaw is negligible compared to that when speaking English. This is why a native-speaker, when using broken-Irish, might say: *'Nil aon "vrakes" ar mo "wicycle"'* ('There are no brakes on my bicycle').

4. Canon O'Leary wrote this and the passages in the following chapter dealing with the same subject when he was 74 years of age, some 35 years

after the events described. If we are to take into consideration a letter he wrote to the society in March 1878, shortly before he was transferred to Macroom, it is obvious that he had become confused as to what really happened. In the letter, he stated that his classes were going ahead well enough and praised the book which he had received from the society. See Appendix 14.

CHAPTER XVI

IN MACROOM

IN the middle of our joy came a change. A letter came from the Bishop telling me to go west to Macroom and do the work of a priest there. That put a stop to the work in Rathcormack. I went west. I wasn't long there when most of my boys followed me. They took lodgings in the village and they'd come to my house every single day. The teaching and learning progressed again.

Some time after this beginning in Macroom, a letter came to me from Dublin, from that 'Society for the Preservation of the Irish Language'. They explained the need for such work as the society was doing and the need for money to carry out the work. Those two points were, without doubt, two bare truths. I sent them a pound and wrote them a letter—and it was in Gaelic that I wrote it.[1] I made an effort in the letter to put before their eyes the right way the work, which they had planned for themselves, ought to be carried out. They sent me an answer, thanking me for the money—and they sent me a copy of the *Freeman's Journal* with my letter in Gaelic, exactly as my hand had parted with it, published in it. However, they gave me to understand concerning the advice I had given them that there was no necessity for haste; it was the same as if they had said: 'My good man, you take care of your own business and let us do the same.'

It wasn't said as bluntly as that, but that was its essence. I didn't blame them at all. Nobody can possibly understand the right way of keeping Gaelic alive if he doesn't know what kind of thing is the living Gaelic. They didn't understand what kind of thing the living Gaelic is, nor what kind is the dead Gaelic. They had it fixed in their minds that they understood those two things far better than I did any one of them. Because of that, they were unable to accept advice from me concerning them and I had no blame for them. But I didn't interfere with them any more with letters—or with money. It was Fr John Nolan, an Order priest, who was at the head of that Society. Without a doubt, he was a very fine, very holy, very goodhearted priest. He did a great deal of work for the sake of Gaelic, and it was hard work. But what is the use of hard work without knowledge?

There was a men's club in Macroom that time; I think they were

'The Young Men's Society'. Some of them saw my Gaelic letter in the *Freeman*. They came and asked me if I would come to their room for a little while every night to try and teach them Gaelic. I said I would, and I came.[2] I was not two minutes in the room, talking to them, when I saw that they had already got a good knowledge of the tongue and that I had nothing to do but to show them how to read and write it. Everybody got pen, ink and paper and the work began. As soon as they had the letters, they would sit up to the table and I would begin telling some story, which they'd write down, every word just as it came from my mouth.

The business didn't cause me much trouble. I didn't have to visit them except on a couple of nights a week, and I'd only wait a half-hour each night. I didn't have to do any oral teaching: the majority had the spoken tongue as well as I had it myself.

The work was proceeding in that manner, easily and light-heartedly. Two or three of the boys from the neighbourhood had come to me to learn Latin, after they had promised to abstain from all alcoholic drink. However, in the middle of our work, there came a thwarting disaster. The parish priest spoke to me, giving me to understand that he didn't like me to be teaching the boys.[3] I told him, nicely and quietly, that it was inside in my own house that I was teaching and that I might as well be doing so as playing cards or falling asleep.

Some time later, a letter came to me from the Bishop, telling me that a parish priest, north in Ráth Luirc[4] greatly desired to found a Latin school in the place.

'There is some money to be had from the Government,' said the Bishop to me, 'to keep up a school of this sort in the place. That money is lying idle at present, since there's no school. I thought it would be a good thing for you to go north to Charleville and do the same work as you've been doing in Macroom.'

I knew what was behind the talk. I knew that the Bishop wouldn't speak like that unless the parish priest of Macroom had complained about me and my school. But I let it go with him.

'Good, my Lord Bishop,' I said. 'Send me north.'

It struck me, also, that perhaps it was the will of God that I go north. I would have greatly preferred to have remained on in Macroom if I'd been left there, but I understood that this was not, perhaps, the will of God. I understood that God might have determined on some work for me to do in Ráth Luirc, which I would not be able to do in Macroom. That is the truth. There was a loneliness on me because I had to leave, for, however short was the time I had been there, myself and the people had a great liking for one and other. I had one satisfaction of mind when I was going away: it was not following my own way I was, but putting my will with the will of God.

'How do I know,' I said in my own mind, 'what God has planned with this business? It wasn't to follow my own will that He made a priest of me!'

I wouldn't say this much about it now, but to show that it would not be right to place any blame on the parish priest of Macroom. If it was the will of God that I went north to Ráth Luirc there was nothing that parish priest did, likewise, but that which the will of God allowed him to do. The poor fellow didn't escape from all the talk the people had about the affair. There was a half-wit in the village, who heard the people talking and saying that the parish priest had got rid of the young priest because of his teaching Latin to the boys.

'It's a strange thing!' said the *amadán*. 'What harm was it for the young priest to be teaching boys? If it was teaching young girls he was, it'd be right, maybe, to tell him not to be doing it—but teaching boys!'

People used to be telling what the fool had said, and they'd have a bit of a laugh. They quickly said that the *amadán* was right, and the old proverb was recalled: 'A thorn in dung, the tooth of a hound, the saying of a fool—the three sharpest things in existence.'

NOTES TO CHAPTER XVI

1. The society had the letter, with a translation, printed in the *Irishman*. See Appendix 14 for this and for evidence that the Canon had obviously become confused as to the true facts of his dealings with the society.
2. The Irish group prospered well. In 1905, Macroom could still be described as 'the most Gaelic town in Co Cork'. By that time, the Gaelic Society ('Cumann na nGael') had become influenced by the Sinn Féin movement and was very active. It could also boast that it was in this town the first feis had been held and the first Irish-language drama had been staged. When money came from Tomás Ó Concheanainn in Mexico to be used for the purpose of prize-money for 'compositions and recitations in the language', the organizers decided on Macroom 'as an Irish-speaking centre; and lo, the recitation competition developed into an Oireachtas for that part of the country' (1898). The following year, the Macroom Players asked Canon O'Leary to write a play for them in Irish, the first in the language; and so 'Tadhg Saor' was performed in August 1900.

Some of O'Leary's relations were very active in the language movement in the area, especially a cousin, Diarmuid O Laoghaire, essayist, folklorist and teacher. It is interesting to note that a nephew taught Irish in the national school in 1905, but was getting no encouragement from the priest of the parish. Nine years later, one year after *Mo Scéal Féin* was written, the parish priest had a school without Irish on the curriculum—evidently a source of satisfaction to him. The Gaelic League, however, started evening classes in Irish in the town.

3. The fact that he was holding Irish classes had, of course, something to do with it, but this was doubtless only fuel to the fire. The curate was still under middle-age and he was an innovator—to his seniors a reformer who was showing them up and a crank.

Canon Sheehan's *My New Curate* highlights a somewhat similar situation with great good humour. Two parish priests are speaking in the passage, one taking the other to task: 'To be very plain with you, your parish is going to the dogs. You are throwing up the sponge and letting this young man do what he likes. Now, I can tell you the people don't like it, the priests don't like it, and when he hears it, as he is sure to hear it, the Bishop won't like it either. . . . We don't want young mashers coming around here to teach old priests their business. We kept the faith—'

The other parish priest, whose new curate has been the cause of the outburst, is a little worried and not a little amused. To himself he muses wryly: 'Clearly something should be done, and done quickly. There was a good deal of talk abroad, and I was supposed to be sinking into senile incompetence. It is quite true that I could not challenge my curate's conduct in a single particular. . . . But it wouldn't do. Everyone said so; and, of course, every one in these cases is right.'

4. Canon O'Leary referred affectionately to the town as 'an Ráth', but the common name for it in those days was Charleville. After the war of independence, however, the town reverted to the original Gaelic name of Ráth Luirc.

CHAPTER XVII

THE SCHOOL IN RÁTH LUIRC

I GATHERED together my furniture and books, and away with me to the north. I went to speak to the parish priest. He told me how everything was to be arranged. In a room in my own dwelling-house, the school was to be. Every one of the scholars would pay ten and twenty in the season, i.e. six pounds in the year. The day's work would start at ten in the morning and finish at two in the day. The money, which the scholars paid, would be put in the kitty along with the offerings, and would be divided among the priests in exactly the same manner as the offerings were; in that way, I would get my share of both it and the offerings. The other priests would have to do the parish work, but I would not have to do anything only the school work.

I listened to these arrangements, without so much as one word coming out of my mouth. The school was opened. Some boys came; I put them working. At the end of a few days, some of my own boys came to me—two or three from Rathcormack, a person from Macroom, and Terence Shealy from Mitchelstown. They got lodgings for themselves in the village. I put them into the work, each according as it suited him.

Here was the work going ahead then—but one thing was bothering me. I had seen how exact the parish priest was about the money, and it set me thinking. As soon as I could, I took my chance to talk over with him the thought which was in my head.

'Just this much, Father,' I said to him. 'Some boys have come after me here. I was teaching them in Macroom and Rathcormack. There was never a mention of money between us, of course. The teaching they will get here must be given to them for nothing, just as they were getting it in the other places.'

He shook his head. 'Oh,' he said, 'that wouldn't do the job at all. They must pay now, like any other scholar coming to the school.'

I stopped, and I must confess my blood stirred. I would have made short work of him, if it hadn't been for just one thing. If it hadn't been for that, I'd have said something like this to him: 'If that's what's in your mind as regards the school, some other person must be found to teach it.'

I didn't say it; I kept it inside. I put a bridle on my anger. When I had my hand firmly on the bridle, I spoke like this: 'Good enough, Father. But, since it was the Bishop sent me here, the Bishop must settle this point between us.'

When the Bishop came, the story was told to him. On the spot, he said I was right.

A person might say, perhaps: 'Why didn't you give up the business immediately, when you were asked to do such a mean stunt?'

I'll tell you. I've already said how we had the library in Kilworth, and the other library, the brass band and music in Rathcormack, all under the protection of St Brigid. The entire business was under her protection. As soon as I opened the school in Ráth Luirc, I put it and myself and everything that had to do with us—the total abstinence movement, especially—under the same protection. It was St Brigid, 'The Mary of the Gaeil', who caused me to press down upon my anger that time, when I was asked to do such a mean stunt. The day after that, I wasn't able to keep in the laughter when I'd think of how little the poor priest knew that he had a right to be grateful to St Brigid that I didn't throw the school at him and say to him: 'If you want to make money out of it, teach it yourself! Do the work yourself!'

Besides, I had another reason for not throwing up the school. I wanted to complete the course for the boys who had followed me. If I had thrown up the school, I would have reneged on them. That would also have been mean. I don't know if they'd sooner pay than have me give up, but I think they would have preferred to do so. But whether they would or they wouldn't, I wasn't going to take any money from them.

Outside of that again, I had got to know some of the boys from the village and the neighbourhood, and found out that they had high intelligence. I realized that it would be worthwhile taking a good deal of trouble with them. I would press back a lot of anger sooner than stop teaching lads so good at taking in knowledge. Outside of that entirely, there was the promise of total abstinence made by each boy who had come to me from the place. If I were to get out of the work there would be every danger that the promise would come to naught in the minds of a lot of those who had made it. There was yet another hold on me as well: I could not put aside the work I had been doing so long before that in honour of St Brigid, in honour of the Mary of the Gaeil. Without a doubt, the people who saw me doing that work were surprised, but they didn't realise the holds that were on me. It had been arranged that I

would not have to do any part of the parish work, but that
arrangement meant nothing: I did my share as well as anyone. I
think a lot of people thought I was silly, and it was no wonder that
they were saying it. But they didn' realize the holds that were on
me.

But, *'fágaimís siúd mar atá sé!'* We'll leave that as it is!

CHAPTER XVIII

THE LAND LEAGUE

I THINK it was just when I was leaving Macroom that Michael Davitt[1] was let out of prison. There came a very wet Summer and a very wet Autumn. There was no chance of paying the rents. Some of the landlords west in Connacht realised that the farmers would be looking for an abatement. They sent out a call to one another and came together in the one spot, where they agreed that no abatement was to be given to any tenant. I recall a great sorrow and uneasiness coming over me when I heard that news. I knew that there was no chance of paying the rents and I reckoned that all the people would be thrown out of their lands and that we would again have the destruction which was done in Ireland in the year of forty-eight. That thought used to be taking the sleep of the night from me.

But it wasn't long until another story came to us from the west. Michael Davitt saw what the landlords had done. he sent out a call to the tenants, asking them to come together in the one spot. They came. He spoke to them. The result of his speech was that they agreed not to give a ha'penny rent to any landlord who would not give a good abatement. That was the twirl to the landlords' twist!

The landlords themselves realised this and they were raging. Davitt was taken and struck into prison again; he had only been out on ticket-of-leave. His ticket was now broken and he was back in again. But, often, things don't turn out as expected. Disraeli was Prime Minister when Davitt's ticket was broken. Three weeks after that, exactly, Disraeli and his crowd were thrown out of the Government, and Gladstone went in. The minute Gladstone was in, the door of the prison opened again and Davitt was let out. It was then that the struggle began between the tenants and the landlords.

This all lifted the great uneasiness from me, but all the same, I was not without fear: I was afraid the tenants would not have the courage to stand their ground. I was afraid that they would believe that they'd have no chance of keeping the rent back without the sheriff coming and throwing them out. When they saw Michael Davitt come out of prison, in spite of the landlords, they were hardly able to believe it. It was not long until he was over in the

west again among them, telling them how they would fight the
landlords. It was extremely hard to convince them that the war was
possible at all. It was rooted in their minds that the landlord had
nothing to do but to come along and throw them out as soon as
they'd refuse to pay the rent.

'If you go to him person by person, he will be able to throw ye
out, person by person. He will be able to throw out on the spot any
person who refuses. But if every group of tenants goes together,
who will he be able to throw out? He won't be able to accuse one
person more than the next. He can't put the law on all of ye at
once. Let the group go to him and offer him the rent—minus the
abatement they want. If he refuses to give the abatement, let the
group leave him—without giving him any rent at all. Many of the
landlords are in need of money and they'll be glad to give the
abatement for the purpose of getting the rent immediately.'

But at first, it wasn't a terribly great opinion some of them had of
this advice. They'd the habit of always giving the landlord his own
way, of giving any rent which would be asked of them sooner than
have the fear of eviction taking the night's sleep from them. But
there were some, as well, who, whatever might come out of it for
them, would prefer to make any sort of fight than to be slaving to
make money for idle people and handing out money that they
themselves were in need of. The Land League[2] was founded. Bit by
bit, the work spread until there was a band of the League in every
parish.

Early on, it was founded in Ráth Luirc. I recall the day well.
There was a big gathering of people in a field, not far from my
school, and myself and the scholars went to it.

When I went in among the people, certain thoughts came to my
mind. I remembered the time I was inside in the college in
Maynooth, when that paper in Dublin was coming down heavily on
myself and the rest of us, saying that we were taking part with the
powers of England. We knew in our hearts that it was calumny, that
we were not taking part with the powers of England but with our
own people, the Irish people, trying to keep them from going into a
conflict with England while they had all the arms and the Irish had
nothing but empty hands. We knew right well that if the people of
Ireland went into a struggle of this sort, there could only be the one
end—a bloody battle perhaps, and then the informer and the
gallows, the blood-money and transportation, and the broken
hearts of fathers and mothers and families in the homes. We knew
right well that if the Irish people had seven times as many weapons

as they had, that if they had as much arms and wealth and numbers as would have kept them going for twenty years, England would lose all she had in the world from her hide out—she would lose her hide itself! she would lose her soul!—sooner than let the Irish people get the upper hand. Where was the wealth? Where was the ammunition? Where were the big guns, or the small guns? Where were the numbers of soldiers? Where was there anything at all which would give the people of Ireland the means of standing a struggle of this sort against England?[3]

But when this struggle between tenants and landowners came, the story was altogether changed. From this on, it wasn't blades or blood, powder or fire, big guns or little, that was in question, but a case of every one keeping his grip on that which was his own. A person doesn't break the law of God or of the realm when all he does is to keep that which is his own. Such was the doctrine given that day from the platform to the people in the field outside Ráth Luirc.

Neither when I was in the college nor when I had come out, had I any power to take a part with the Fenians or give them any council which would further their activities; but there was nothing to prevent me giving advice to a congregation of farmers and telling them to go ahead with their movement. I realised that they were in need of council. They were all about me—sullen and dejected. The ancient terror still! The fear that they would be seized shortly and the law brought to bear on them, as was always usual, the fear that they would not come off scot-free, although they had broken neither the law of God nor that of the realm. I was looking at them: I saw the dejection, the terror, the mistrust in themselves and in each other on their faces. Everyone terrified for fear that the master would be told that he was in the field on that day!

There was nobody on the platform yet, but four or five young lads. Then a strong young priest from County Limerick came and went up on the platform. I myself went up with him. He began to speak, and he was right good at it. He spoke boldly, explaining how the masters were doing an injustice to the farmers when they demanded rents that could not be made out of the land. The farmers, listening to the speech, were amazed that someone had the nerve to tell the truth so outspokenly. As he was speaking, I was looking at them. More priests came. Every one, as he came, leaped up until there were so many of us there was hardly room for any more.

Here's something I noticed that day, which has never since

parted from my memory and never will: when the people saw the crush of priests up on the platform and each priest, as his turn came, speaking more boldly and dauntlessly than the person before him, the dejection, fear and mistrust began to go out of their faces. I was able to read the face of each one of them, exactly as if he had spoken to me: 'Yes! As long as those priests are all up there on the platform, there's no danger to us!' When I saw that much, there was a great gladness on me and I was very grateful to the priests for coming and standing there between the poor farmers and the cut-throats who were squeezing the souls out of them.

Along with that, there was another great gladness on me, with an even greater cause for it! At long last, the whole world was able to see that the reason the priests had been against the Fenians was not from any affection for the English nor for their laws; and that a terrible injustice was done to them when the opposite was said.

NOTES TO CHAPTER XVIII

1. Some historians would hold—with at least some degree of justification—that Michael Davitt did more towards the shaping of this modern Ireland than any other single person in the last 100 years. Born of Irish-speaking parents in Straide, Co Mayo in 1846, he went to work in a cotton-mill in Manchester at the age of ten, following the eviction and emigration of his family. He lost an arm in a machine and, because of this, received an education he would not otherwise have been given. He became organising secretary of the Fenian Brotherhood in Britain and was sentenced to 15 years penal servitude for sending arms to Ireland. Released on ticket-of-leave, he went to work immediately to link revolutionary Fenianism with constitutional agitation—the now-famous 'New Departure'. He began the Land War, founded the Land League, put Parnell in the driver's seat of the new movement. It is only now, almost a century later, when small farms are proving uneconomic, that his ideas on land nationalisation—he was against peasant ownership—are being proven correct. He opposed Parnell during the 'split', later became an M.P. and joined with William O'Brien in founding the United Irish League. His later political career, now too often forgotten, was one which commands the highest respect. He died in 1906. For a useful essay on his life, see: J. W. Boyle (Ed.) *Leaders and Workers*. Mercier Press, Cork, 1966.
2. The Land War dates from 1879, when Davitt, with the help of local Fenians, organised an agrarian demonstration in his native Irishtown, in Mayo. Canon O'Leary omits any mention of the fact that the landlord in question was the local parish priest, Canon Burke. It is only fair to add that the Roman Catholic parish clergy backed the League solidly and were a powerful factor in its success.

It is interesting to note that although, in its early days, the bulk of the new resistance was Irish-speaking, the League seems to have been always referred to under its English title. Even Canon O'Leary in *Mo Scéal Féin* never calls it by anything else. Neither, in fact, does he give Michael Davitt his correct Gaelic patronymic but speaks of 'Micheál Daibhéid'.

3. It is ironic to remember that within three years of writing this the Canon was to witness a rebellion of the sort he here condemns. In his own parish of Castlelyons, the Kent family by themselves rose out in rebellion in support of the Dublin insurgents. The farmhouse siege, in retrospect, seems more reminiscent of the Appalachian Mountains than of the quiet Cork country-side. One brother was killed; and another executed in Cork prison on 9 May, 1916—Thomas Kent, one of the 'Sixteen Dead Men' of 1916. The Kents' gallant farmhouse-rebellion is almost forgotten today, but there is a shot-by-shot account of it to be found under the title of *The Kents of Bawnard* by Patrick J. Power in *Rebel Cork's Fighting Story,* Anvil Books, Tralee.

Canon O'Leary had founded a branch of the Gaelic League in Castle-lyons. The Kents were most enthusiastic members.

CHAPTER XIX

A CHANGE IN THE WORLD

A BRANCH of the Land League was now founded in Charleville. A couple of days a week, the farmers would come in from the neighbourhood and everyone of them would pay a small piece of money towards the costs of the group. It was only a little bit but they were slow enough to pay it until the reports started to appear in the newspapers of certain events happening throughout the country.

There was a report about the action of tenants in one place. The master had sent his messenger to them as usual, to tell them brusquely to come on a certain day and pay the rent. They went on the day that was named—but they all went into the master together and told him that they wouldn't give any rent to him if they didn't get a twenty-five per cent abatement—the fourth penny or a crown in the pound. He flew into a rage and said that he wouldn't give as much as a ha'penny. They listened to him quietly until the outburst was over. Then, there was a great contention and argument between themselves and himself. At last, he knocked off the fifth penny for them, i.e. twenty per cent or four shillings in the pound.

When this report was read out of the paper to them, everyone stared in open-mouthed astonishment and drew a fine, long breath. They were all surprised and amazed. Within a few days, another report of the same kind was read out. In a week, another report. *Ach aidhe!* From that out, you'd see the hand of every one of them down in a pocket of his breeches with alacrity and the bright money coming on the table to us in heaps!

They had the surprise of their lives; they had never heard of such a thing before. Law and imprisonment, eviction and taking possession, and the going off to a life of cold and wandering—that was what they had thought would come from refusing to pay the rent, and here was a crown in the pound for some and four shillings in the pound for others as the outcome! What about that for a change in the world?

I myself thought back on the times I had put behind me, on Saunders and Broderick, on the law and the wrangling, and on 'the piece of a goose that was eaten long ago, when it was Christmas'.

Certainly, I gave thanks from the heart to the God of Glory, who had permitted me to live until I saw this change of times, and the routing and defeat of the thieves. We had gained the upperhand as completely as if we had wrought the havoc of Clontarf on them, down on the plains of Kildare!

We had a person down from Kilmallock in the chair for a while. Every time the group would be meeting, he used come down to us. I'd go at times, but I couldn't always do so as I had the responsibility of the school. Everything was going beautifully with us for a while. Then, one day, an account came in the paper of a thing which happened out west in Tralee: the Tralee branch of the Land League were gathered in a room, doing their business when, suddenly and without the slightest expectation of it, a crowd of soldiers leaped in on top of them and all who were there were taken prisoners. That report went throughout Ireland and it left many in the League shaking hand and foot. A couple of days afterwards, the Charleville branch were to meet to do business. They gathered, but the chairman didn't come. They were unable to do any work that day. After night had fallen, who should come into the school to me but the entire band. They sat in the seats, where the boys used to sit during the day. One of them spoke.

'There's something we want of you, Father,' he said, 'and we trust that you won't hold it against us nor refuse us.'

'Good enough,' I said. 'What do ye want?'

'We've no chairman,' he said. 'Would you be willing, Father, to come and be our chairman?'

'Ach! If that's all ye want,' said I, 'it isn't hard to satisfy ye. I reckoned it was something very great ye wanted. I'll come and welcome,' said I. 'When will ye have the next meeting?'

'We'd like to have it tomorrow at six o'clock in the evening, so that you wouldn't be working in the school during it.'

'Good enough,' said I. 'Ye'll have me there at six o'clock tomorrow evening, with God's help.'

At six o'clock on the next evening, I went to the room and we did our business grand and calmly and quietly. Neither peeler nor soldier came to us. And no further news came to us from Tralee. The work went ahead all over the country, the farmers going in groups together demanding abatements and getting them after a dispute; the courage of the people was blooming and strengthening by the day.

The parish priest, however, had no affection for the Land League. He was old. Probably, the poor person thought the Land

League was only the Fenians under another name and that their counsel was an evil one. Whatever he thought, he had no love for the business. I think that he wrote to the Bishop asking him to counsel me and to tell me that the responsibility of the school was large enough for me, without having the responsibility of the Land League along with it. A letter came from the Bishop saying that he was afraid some of the boys would stay away from the school because I was immersed in the League. I wrote to him and I said something like this:

'My Lord Bishop,' I said, 'instead of it doing any damage to the school, my being in the Land League will benefit it. All the boys, who are coming to the school, are from farming families with the exception of two and the fathers of this pair themselves have a great affection for the Land League.'

'And there is another thing, my Lord Bishop,' I said. 'If I had told those, who came to me that night to ask me to be their director, that I could not do it because the responsibility of the school was enough for me, what do you suppose they would say? They would say that it was because I was afraid of the peelers. Wouldn't that be a nice thing for me then? Especially when I wasn't afraid, nor anything of the sort? How could I look those men in the eye ever again, if I had showed cowardice that time? Especially when there was no cowardice in me?'

I got no more 'counsel' from the Bishop. That didn't surprise me at all. I wasn't doing anything but that which he would have done himself, if he had been in my place. He was a McCarthy. It would not have been according to his kind to have any cowardice in him; and there wasn't,

The school work and the other work proceeded together, and we were putting life behind us. The parish priest used entertain a bit. He'd often have myself and the other young priest to dinner. One day, we were at dinner in his house with six or seven others, who, for the most part, were people who had as little love for the Land League as had the man of the house. The talk went among them like this:

'Isn't it on his word that everybody lives? When a person makes a bargain, isn't it right for him to stand by his bargain? When a farmer makes a bargain with a landlord and when he promises to pay a certain amount of rent out of a farm of land, isn't he bound to pay that rent or give back the land to the person who owns it?'

Anger was rising in me and I listening to that kind of talk. At last I spoke.

'I would like to put a question to you, Father,' I said to the man of the house, 'if you please.'

'Oh, put it, put it, Father,' he said.

'I knew a man,' I said, 'who had a farm of land and there was fifty pounds rent to be paid out on it. He had a lease on the farm. The lease expired about a dozen years ago. The master came to him. "You've had this farm at fifty pounds a year for a long time" he said. The other man didn't say a word. "From this on you must pay a hundred pounds rent a year," the master said. The other man didn't say a word. "You've made a new house here," said the master. "Probably you lost a couple of hundred pounds on it. You'll be allowed two hundred for whatever you lost on it. At five pounds in the hundred, that would come to ten pounds a year. The rent will be lowered by that much to you. That leaves you with ninety pounds rent a year from this on. Are you satisfied with that?" The other man didn't say a word. The master stopped for a while, waiting to see what the tenant would say. But he didn't say a word. At last, the master spoke again. "It doesn't matter to me in the devil whether you're satisfied or not," he said, "but that's the rent you'll have to pay from this on!" Would you call such dealings a bargain, Father?' I asked the parish priest.

It's probable there was an edge to my voice, for neither himself nor anyone else spoke for a while.

'Oh,' said he, at last, 'that's a special case.'

'It is not, Father,' said I 'It is a common case. For some forty years, I have been looking at land business between masters and tenants and I have never yet seen an alternative to that type of bargain being made between them. I never saw anything except rents being raised every time a lease fell due or every single time a tenant would make any improvement on his farm with his own hands.'

There was a little, hawk-like, crooked-eyed man-een sitting in front of me, over on the other side of the table. He looked across at me and he spoke.

'And, Father,' said he, 'if he wasn't satisfied to pay out ninety pounds for the farm, why did he not speak out and say that he wasn't satisfied?'

'That's fine, a *mhic-ó*,' said I to him. 'If he had said that he wasn't satisfied, he'd have been thrown out of the house he had built for himself and his wife and family. Then, I suppose, you'd have given him shelter!'

He didn't speak any more. For the rest of the evening, some other subject of talk was drawn down—they had had enough of that same bargain, the one-sided one, 'the hag's division—as she wants it herself'.

An Order priest came to the town to give a mission. He saw the school—'St Brigid's School' was the name I had on it. It pleased him greatly. He got to know some of the boys. He himself had founded a school down in Limerick city, to teach boys and make priests out of them (if it were God's will) and to send them over to foreign places, spreading the faith. He was a Ronan. He used to say that he had great faith in the poor boys of Ireland, there was such great stuff in them and they having descended from the dynasties of Éire; that they had the noble drop although they had not worldly riches; that they made better priests than the offspring of our wealthy people, because they had a natural nobility of mind, despite their lack of wealth. 'The Apostolic School' was the name Fr Ronan had on his school. My boy, Terence Sheeley, was sent to meet him. They got to know each other. When Fr Ronan was going away, Terence went with him.

Fr Ronan was in the Jesuits. He put Terence into the Apostolic School. The boy is now a priest, in the Company of Jesus over in America and he is a credit to the Jesuits, to his people, to his native country, and to me, since it was I laid the first hand on him.[1]

There was another boy I had in the school. He belonged to the area and his name was Daniel Mannix. He is now the Archishop over in Melbourne.[2] A lot of the boys whom I had at school are after getting ahead well, some as priests, some in other worthy vocations.

NOTES TO CHAPTER XIX

1. 'In 1880, Father William Ronan, S. J., had started an Apostolic School in the Crescent College, Limerick. The school was a remarkable success from the beginning. . . . It was decided to re-open Mungret College, and to combine in one establishment the Apostolic School and the Diocesan Seminary. On 14 September, 1882, Mungret College was opened formally by the Jesuit Fathers. The College opened with about sixty students of whom half belonged to each school.' (*Irish Jesuit Directory and Year Book*, 1944.)

Rev. Terence J. Shealey, S. J., ('one of the earliest and certainly one of the most distinguished of the past pupils of the Apostolic school', according to the Mungret Annual, 1923) became the first Dean of the Law School at Fordham University, New York, and also filled the Chair of Professor of

Jurisprudence for many years. He was a famous preacher, established the Spritual Retreats for Laymen at Fordham College and was the Director of Staten Island Retreat House for 13 years. The old Canon could well have felt proud that such an influential career had its beginnings in his humble Classical schools.

2. Dr Daniel Mannix, Archbishop of Melbourne for close on half a century, is celebrated for his patriotic services to his native land. Once, the British Government sent a warship to arrest him on the high seas because they feared his landing in Ireland would have caused undesirable (from their point of view!) political repercussions.

Before going to Australia, he had been President of Maynooth College—another tribute to O'Leary's Classical schools—and, in that position, welcomed his old mentor after he had received the Freedom of Dublin in 1913. Dr Mannix's presidency, however, affords a good example of just how entangled Irish national aspirations were in the first quarter of this century. He publicly expressed his dissatisfaction with both the 1916 Rebellion and the 1921 Truce! He was opposed to compulsory Irish in the National University and clashed with Dr Michael O'Hickey, Professor of Irish in Maynooth and one of the great advocates of the proposal. The episode came to a sorry conclusion—so much so that, 15 years later, John Devoy the Fenian could write: 'If Archbishop Mannix lives a hundred years and did penance in sackcloth and ashes for his crime against Ireland, he ought never to be forgiven.'

CHAPTER XX

INJUSTICE, VENGEANCE AND COERCION

Here's a question: how did it come about that the farmers were able to inflict such a defeat on the landlords at the time? This is the answer: Gladstone was the cause of it.[1]

Long before, Gladstone had seen the Irish farmers under the iron heel of the landlords. By dint of ingenuity and adroitness, he put a law through the Parliament in the year 1870,[2] which aimed at forcing any landlord, who would put out a tenant, to make restitution to him for taking away his dwelling-place. The landlords made a right cod of that law. In spite of Gladstone and his law, they continued to throw people out and to send them to a life of cold and wandering. Then, Gladstone refused to give them any assistance against the Land League, when it had risen against them. That's what killed them. The farmers were doing nothing against the law; they were only refusing to pay a rent that was too high and which was put on them against their will. Gladstone could not appreciate that anyone should be forced to help the landlords obtain this rent when they themselves had shown that they had no respect for the law, by making a cod of the restitution act. Without assistance from the government, they had no chance of obtaining any kind of rent at all; they were in a bad way. If things had gone on in that manner, the farmers would have had every single thing as they wanted it—but things didn't!

A rule had been made by the Land League, when a farmer would be put out of his land for being unable to pay rack-rent, that no other person was to take his farm. This is the rule that broke the landlords' hearts. If the procedure was done exactly according to the rule, there was no use in any landlord throwing out a tenant for the land would be left idle on his hands. In places, the rule was kept well enough, but it was broken here and there, where there was a man to be found who would yield to greed and take a farm from which another had been put out. That would send the evicted man into a red rage. Without a doubt, it would be hard to do a more detestable apostasy than that. The outcome was that in places revenge was taken on the grabber. That was the first turning-point for the better that the landlords got. They knew that Gladstone had to put the law into force against such vengeance, and they were exultant.

According as acts of vengeance of this kind were done, the news would be told all over England and exaggerated beyond all bounds. When a landlord had a farm on his hands, after he had thrown out some poor person, he'd be on the look-out for an avaricious man to come to him and take it. If he came, the farm would be given very cheaply to him, on purpose so as to make naught of the League rule, if that were possible. At times, the farm would be given to the avaricious one for a year or two without any rent, for the same reason—but this would be done in secret. The acts of vengeance increased because of this chicanery. People were injured. Then, people were killed. Gladstone couldn't let this type of thing go on. The landlord did not break the law of the realm when he threw out the tenant—no more than he broke the law when he did his best to put another tenant into the farm. The avaricious man did not break the law of the realm when he took the farm; without a doubt, he broke the moral law, when he did a thing to his neighbour that he would not like the neighbour to do to himself; the farm belonged to his neighbour, because it was through an injustice that he had been put out of it. The law did not defend him against this injustice, but that did not make a right of wrong. Nevertheless, the neighbour broke both the law of God and the law of the realm at the one time when he put a bullet through the grabber for taking his farm from him.[3]

About this time, I saw a paper, called *Punch*, over from London. There used to be funny pictures in it, but if they were funny itself, they'd have a deep meaning at times. In the paper I saw, there was this picture: Gladstone, in a peeler's uniform, standing bolt upright in front of a shop, with his back to the door and he looking away from him to the bottom of the sky; inside the shop, at the counter, were men with black cloth on their faces buying arms, guns and pistols, swords and pikes; a priest within at the counter and he selling the arms to them; and there was Disraeli outside with Gladstone, looking up at him with his finger pointed towards the shop and this talk, as it were, coming from his mouth, 'I say, Mr Pleeceman, I think it is about time that you should look in here!'

Then, one after another, came the coercive laws, every one of them sharper than the one before, until honest men from all over Ireland were stuck into the prisons, without a trial of law, without the judgement of the twelve—and until such time as Gladstone pronounced that famous saying, 'The resources of civilisation are not yet exhausted.'

In every place, money was being got together for the people who were in prison. I thought of a way to make some money for those men from Charleville who were inside. I decided to make a sort of raffle; here are the prizes which were on the raffle tickets:

A splendid Bengal tiger called 'Resources of Civilisation'. Warranted sound in wind and limb.

A huge African elephant called 'Passive Resistance'.

An Egyptian mummy called 'Rackrent', said to be as old as the days of Moses.

A magnificent puck goat called 'Peel', alias 'Fix Bayonets'.

With many other highly interesting and valuable prizes.

The tickets were sold quickly. The parish priest saw one of them. He was raging. He came to me with a ticket in his hand.

'It was yourself put these out, Father,' he said.

'It was myself, without a doubt,' I said. 'Don't you see my name down on them?'

'And what are they for?' he asked.

'To make money.'

'And what's the money for?'

'Since you put the question to me, I'll tell you exactly,' said I. 'To send it to the men from this village, whom Buckshot has inside in prison.'

There was anger in the voice of each of us, while we were talking. It wasn't long afterwards that the Bishop sent me east to Kilworth in place of the parish priest who was there, for the poor person was very old and leaving his senses and he wasn't suitable for the work.

NOTES TO CHAPTER XX

1. Reservation or, even, speciousness has not been the least conspicuous mark of the Irish clergy during the past century or more! There were historic causes for this, of course, and Canon O'Leary was no different from his contemporaries. Mr Gladstone was indeed 'the Friend of Ireland', but to give him all the credit was too much. The two men foremost in the 'Fall of Feudalism in Ireland' were Michael Davitt and Charles Stewart Parnell. Davitt, in the eyes of the Catholic Church, was tainted with Socialism and Fenianism; Parnell was a name the clergy did their best to tear out from the pages of history.

2. Gladstone was barely in office when he introduced and carried the first of many Land Acts. This one legalised the 'Ulster custom', which secured

the tenant as long as he paid his rent and enabled him to sell his interest in his farm. It had little effect. Another act eleven years later gave the tenants 'the three F's—fair rent, fixity of tenure and free sale'. By then, however, it was clear to their leaders that the tenant must become the owner of his land. It was not until the Wyndham act of 1903 that the old landlordism was abolished and Ireland became a land of peasant proprietors.

3. In the year 1880 alone, there were 2,590 'agrarian outrages'. On the other hand, between 1874 and 1881, there were some 10,000 evictions.

The Coercion Act in the early part of 1881 only served to intensify agrarian crime. It is difficult for us to realise the appalling state of affairs until we glance at some of the figures submitted by Sir Charles Russell to the Parnell Commission. The figures are for the whole of Ireland in 1882:

Murders	26
Firing at persons	58
Firing into dwellings	117
Incendiary fires and arson	281
Cattle outrages	144

CHAPTER XXI

'BARRY THE RAKE'

WHEN I had settled beyond in Kilworth again, after leaving Rathcormack and the Ráth behind me, I felt my health failing in some way. The people told me I was looking very worn-out. It seems the work had been too hard on me in Ráth Luirc, with the school, the parish work and the work of the Land League all going on at the one time. I didn't take on any more schoolwork. Land League activity was as intense in Kilworth at the time as it was in any part, but, if it was, there were people in charge already and I had nothing to do but go and give advice now and again. This left me without any responsibility but that of the parish and it wasn't long until I was in full strength and full heart again.

I used to be out and about the parish in a little trap that I had, or on horseback. It was a great change from being inside in the school. The people and myself would often meet and it was always Gaelic that we spoke to each other. A little fellow came in from Gortnaskehy to me, one day, to ask me to go and put the oils on a person who was ill in his house. A small, aged man-een, he was. He had come by foot. I knew that he must have been tired, so I put him into the little trap beside me and gave him a lift home. The poor man was very grateful.

We began talking. I started asking him for news of the neighbours, to find out who had gone from here or had died since I left the parish nine or ten years before. In the enquiry, I asked him where was 'Barry the Rake', or was he dead.

'He's dead, the poor man,' said he. 'May his soul be the better for it!'

'Barry the Rake was a poet,' said I.

'He was, to be sure, Father,' he said. 'I came across a bit of poetry he made and, to be sure, he made it very nicely.'

'Tell me it, if you have it,' said I to him.

'I have it, Father,' said he. And this is the story as he told it, in Gaelic:

In the bad times, it was, when the hunger was on everyone. There was a poor fellow, by the name of Sean O'Griffey, living north there on Caherdrinny. The poor fellow wasn't too clever in himself. He was married and there wasn't any great cleverness in the wife, no more than in himself. They'd a daughter and there was less cleverness in that one than there was in either of the pair. Barry the Rake used often go to their house; he knew them well. He'd get lodgings from them at times and a meal of food. There was a parish priest over at Mitchelstown that time (it's likely you remember him, Father), Maurice O'Brien was his name.

Well, the hunger was as bad within in Mitchelstown as it was in any part, for there were a lot of poor people there and they were very badly off. Things were so bad that Father Maurice was buying meal for them and dealing it out among them so that they wouldn't die of the famine. Barry heard that the meal was being given out over in Mitchelstown. He thought—and no wonder—that poor Sean O'Griffey was getting it and that he himself would get a feed of it to eat, if only he went north to Caherdrinny. Off with him to the north and he with the hunger on him. He went into the house.

'Is there anything here a starving man could eat?' he said.

There wasn't one bit of food under the roof of the house.

'I thought ye'd have some of the meal,' said Barry.

'What meal is that?' said Sean.

'This meal that's being given out north there in Mitchelstown.'

'I never heard a word about it,' says Sean.

'May ye roast!' says Barry. 'Go away off north on the spot and bring us some of it.'

'I've no money.'

'The parish priest is giving it away without looking for any money. He's donating it to the poor. Go away on the spot and bring us some of it, I'll stay here 'til you come back. I'm fainting with the hunger.'

Sean went off to the north and, after a good while, he came back. 'Did you bring the meal with you?' Barry asked him.

'I didn't,' says Sean.

'Why not?'

'Because I didn't get it.'

'What was said to you?'

'I was asked was I starving.'

'And what did you say to them?'

'I said I wasn't.'

'*Airiú*, may ye roast!' said Barry. 'Why didn't you tell them the truth?'

'I wouldn't give it to them to be saying it!' said Sean.

'*Ó mhaise,* God be with us! God and Mary be with us!' Barry said.

He drew a pen and a piece of paper from his pocket—he used to have them to be writing the poetry—and sat down and wrote this verse:

> Oh Father Maurice, whose speech is keen and witty,
> Please give some of that meal you have to Sean O'Griffey;
> His wife's a silly fool and his eldest girl's an eegit,
> Himself's a bit of a bags—and will be 'til he deceases.[1]

'Here,' said he to Sean. 'Take this paper-een with you and set off for the priest's own house and give it to him, into his own hand, and you'll get the meal. Go off now and don't be long.'

Sean went away and he took the paper-een with him. He came to the door of the priest's house.

'What do you want?' said the housekeeper.

'I was told to give this paper into the parish priest's own hands,' says Sean.

She snapped the paper out of his hand and away she went inside. 'Here, Father,' she said, 'and the messenger says it must be given into your own hands.'

He read what was in the paper and jumped up from the chair. 'Who gave you this?' he said.

'A poor person that's outside at the door, Father,' said she.

'Send him right into me.'

Sean was sent in. 'Who gave you this paper?' said the priest.

Sean told his story as best he could. 'And are you Sean O'Griffey?' the priest said.

'I am, Father.'

'I understand,' said the priest. The hunger was taken off Sean and he was given as much meal as he could take away with him. 'And,' said the priest to him, 'tell the man who gave you this paper to come here in the morning—I have use for him.'

The next morning, the poet went north to Mitchelstown and he was given his fill to eat; and, when he had eaten his fill, he was given a suit of clothes and told to come again when he had need of food or clothing.

* * *

Anyone, who will read with attention to detail this fragment of poetry that Barry wrote, will see something that is worth his while noting: he will see that there is only a truly small amount of words in the verse, yet that there is as much said there as would not be said in English with seven times the amount of words.

The poet has a favour to ask of Father Maurice. He praises his *guntacht* and his *líomhacht*[2]—a long speech in English would be required to make those two praises, and the long speech itself wouldn't make both praises half as nicely as the two Gaelic words do. Then, the poet has to arouse pity in Father Maurice's heart for Sean O'Griffey. Where is the man living who is a greater pity than he who is married to a silly fool of a woman? If the daughter had any sense, perhaps he'd have things easier, but there was a double misfortune on the poor man when the daughter was a fool as well as the mother. Then, the worst part of it all! 'Himself's a bit of a bags'—and to crown that evil itself, 'he'll be like that 'til he deceases!' It's no wonder that Father Maurice leaped out of his chair when he read the paper!

I know a lot of English poetry and a lot of the poetry of Greece and Rome. In the poetry of any language of them, dead or alive, there is known to me no four lines as good as those four Barry the Rake composed that time when he was starving! *'Brevis esse certo,'* said Horatius, *'et obscurus fio'.* Barry's speech in this verse is as *'brevis'* as it could possibly be, far more pithy than would be possible in any other tongue, and, in place of any *'obscuritas'* arising from the pithyness, there is extra light because of it; it is how the light on the idea is cleaned and strengthened.

NOTES TO CHAPTER XXI

1. A Athair Murchadh, atá go gunta líomhtha,
   Tabhair-se cuid de'n mhín seo do Sheághan ua Gríobhtha;
   Tá a bhean 'na h-óinsigh, agus a inghean chríona,
   Tá sé féin 'na bhreall, agus beidh sé amhlaidh choídhce!

2. *'guntacht'*. In Fr Dineen's dictionary, the meaning is given as 'sharpness, sublety, piquancy, keenness in argument'.
   'líomhacht'. 'Polish, refinement, excellence (of speech, language, etc.)
   The two above qualities are especial characteristics of all Irish poetry, by which even banality may be invested with dignity. In fact, Canon O'Leary bases his criticism of the above *'burdún'* by Barry the Rake wholly on its possession of these qualities—both of which are virtually impossible to carry over into an English translation.
   Two chapters in *A View of the Irish Language* (Brian Ó Cuív, Ed.) are very helpful as regards understanding Irish folk-poetry and the good qualities in folk-speech; they are 'The Gaeltacht' (Caoimhín Ó Danachair) and 'Irish Oral Tradition' (Seán Ó Súilleabháin).

CHAPTER XXII

TENANTS AND LORDS

WHILE I was in Kilworth that time, I kept an eye on the struggle going on between the farmers and the landlords—and a pretty sight it was!

When people would do evil deeds of vengeance on grabbers, who had taken land out of which some tenant had been evicted, the story would be told and enlarged on in the papers over in England. Then, anger would come on the English people and coercive laws would have to be put into force. The landlord would take heart and adopt the old arrogance. He'd send a letter to a tenant, demanding rent from him. The letter would be shown to me. This is the sort of talk that would be in it:

Carey,

    Come in here on Saturday and pay your rent. The next application will be a writ.

        George Smith.

When I saw one of these letters, I advised Carey to go and pay the rent for fear he would incur additional expense. He went in the following Saturday. He drew the full of his fist of money from his pocket and handed it to the agent. This man counted it. It was short some pennies. The agent took up the money in his hand and he dashed it against the wall, so that the pieces went dancing all over the floor.

'Pick it up now,' he said, 'and go and bring me in the full amount!'

Carey picked up the money, put it in his pocket and headed for the door. Just as he was going outside, he said, 'When I give it to you again, you will keep it.'

Home he came. The writ followed. But, if it did itself, he paid no attention to it.

In a little while, there came a change of law. The game went in the tenant's favour and against the landlord. Nothing happened for a time. Then, another letter from the same agent reached Carey:

Dear Mr Carey,

I shall feel much obliged if you will come in next Saturday and let me
have the rent. The amount you owe is—— (without any mention of the
ten-and-forty for the writ).

I remain,

Yours sincerely,

G. Smith.

Carey did not go in and Smith did not get the money, that time
nor ever since.

That's the way the lords used to be, smooth and rough, civil and
churlish every alternate occasion, as the game was going for them
or against them, up or down. They used to remind me of something that happened beside a farmer's house many years before.
There were two beggars in the place; one of them hadn't got the
use of an arm and the other had a leg so shrunken that, when the
poor man was walking, you'd think it was bending and rising he
was. It happened this day that the pair were coming to the
farmer's house at the same time in the evening. They didn't expect
each other and, to be sure, they had no welcome for each other.
Each would have preferred the other not to have come. The man
with the shrunken leg thought that he'd give a sharp, little gibe to
the other man.

'Isn't is strait-handed the weather is with us, Sean!' he said. (The
weather was very broken.)

The word 'strait-handed' stung poor Sean but, if it did, he gave
back a sting every bit as sharp: '*Ach,* it's only up and down, up and
down, *a mhic-ó!*'

It happened that the man of the house was listening to the talk
and he roared out laughing. 'By the deer,' said he, 'but ye gave it to
each other as nicely as ever I heard it done! "Strait-handed" and
"up and down"!'

He got the pair to go inside and to be peaceable with each other.

But that's how the landlords and agents were during that time,
'up and down, up and down, *a mhic-ó',* one day smooth and
another rough, one day civil and another churlish, one day
mannerly and the next bad-mannered, according as the game was
going for them or against them.

It was impossible to convince them that it was not a grievous
injustice to prevent them bringing the law into full play on the
farmers and squeezing the rent from them, even if that meant
squeezing the very life from them along with it. One day, I was at

dinner in the house of a gentleman of the place. There was a landlord at table. Now and again, he was shooting off a word or two about the injustice being done to the poor lords, but I wasn't letting on that I understood what he was going on about. A nice, poor man he was in every other way and I didn't want to be provoking him. There was another gentleman at the table, a doctor, all of whose sympathies, I knew, were with the landlords—it'd be no harm for me to give him a little dig if he were to give me cause and opportunity. This he did. The conversation got onto whether the farmers or the landlords were in the right and how an end could be put to acts of vengeance. I wasn't saying a word. At last, the doctor spoke to me, bluntly and directly.

'Tell me this much, Father,' said he. 'What do ye want?'

He thought that I would give him the opportunity of saying what we wanted was that the land be given to the farmers without rent and that this would violate the seventh commandment, being nothing less than taking a neighbour's portion unlàwfully.

'I'll tell you, doctor, what we want,' said I. 'Here's what we want: that no person should have the power to take and keep another's portion. The fruits of the labour belong to him who labóurs. He, who takes from a person the fruit of his labour, does him an injustice. What we want is that a stop be put to that injustice by law.'

The doctor didn't put a second question to me.

I wasn't but two years in the parish when it was the will of God to call the old priest. Everybody said that it was my right to get the parish then. I didn't get it, however. The Bishop said that he had a mind to give me the parish if the old priest had lived a couple or three more years, but that he couldn't give it to me then as he had many other priests who were a lot longer at the work than I was and it would be an injustice to them to do so. If I had spoken, I would have asked what the reason was that one of them had not been sent to do the work of the parish instead of me. But I did not speak. I didn't say a word. I spent another two years there under the new parish priest, showing him the roads and getting him and the people to know one and other. He hadn't got a word of Gaelic, although it was in the town of Macroom he was reared.

I spent two years in Kilworth with that parish priest and then I was sent north to Doneraile. I wasn't long in the place when war arose between the biggest landlord there—Lord Doneraile was his title—and his tenants. He used to be boasting that he had never evicted a tenant. However, they used to go. Here's how he did the job. He had all the farms set very dearly. When a tenant would come to pay the rent, whatever amount he had to give was accepted, nicely and quietly, and the amount outstanding was put down against him in the account book. The tenant would always pay the highest amount he was able—that is to say, he'd pay more rent than he ought to have done by right. But the account against him would be increasing day by day so that his heart would be broken from thinking on it and he knowing that he'd never have a chance of cleaning that book. The story would slip out. The neighbours would know of the big amount of money in the book against the man. Among the neighbours, there'd be one who'd have some sum of money saved up, from the grazier business perhaps, and who'd hear the story of this farm. He'd come to talk to the agent.

'It's like this, sir,' he'd say. 'I heard that farm of Sean Thingummy's was to be set and, the way things are, the place would suit me very well.'

'The farm isn't to be set yet,' the agent would say, 'but the rent is four hundred pounds in arrears. The master only wants what is his. He doesn't wish to be too hard on poor Sean Thingummy but everybody must get what is theirs. If you pay the four hundred pounds, you'll get the farm at at the same rent as Thingummy.'

'Good enough, sir,' the man with the money would say and off he'd go.

The agent would send for Sean Thingummy. Poor Sean would come, shaking hand and foot. 'It's like this, Sean', the agent would say. 'Your rent is four hundred pounds in arrears in the book.'

'It is in truth, sir,' Sean would say.

'Here's the way things are, Sean. The master doesn't wish to be hard on you. If he wanted to, he could take all you have by right of law, and evict you without a farthing. He doesn't wish to do that on you and your wife and family. He'd be satisfied if you left the place and took all you have with you. You've a mare and three head of cattle and a couple of sheep. The law would allow him to take these from you if he so wished, but he'd be satisfied if you took them and gave him possession. But you know yourself that if things go to law everything in the place will be taken off you.'

Sean Thingummy would understand what the meaning of this talk was. He'd give away his possession and take with him whatever little effects he had. His four hundred pounds would be re-mitted—and, of course, the master was a 'big-hearted' man for 'remitting' it! The man with the money would get the farm and the master would get that four hundred pounds which was remitted to Sean Thingummy.

But the man with the money might, perhaps, have only three hundred. He'd get the other hundred on loan from the bank; this would put an extra six pounds a year on his rent, one that was already too high by far. Until he'd have put in, maybe, nine or ten years at it, he'd keep on breaking his heart working the farm. They'd never be too hard on him about rent, but, when he'd have spent a few years in the place, there would be, in spite of his life-and-death effort, another four hundred pounds in the book against him.

Then, exactly the same game in the same manner would be played. Again, the four hundred pounds would be 'remitted' to yet another moneyed-man when it could be had from him. They were coming and going after one and other, just like that! That's the story which was told to me when I went to Doneraile and was trying to discover how things were there.

The contention arose because the tenants wanted a reduction in the rent, just the same as tenants were getting on every other estate in the locality. Lord Doneraile would give no reduction away. All the tenants came to me to ask me to take the money into my own hands—that is, the rent money minus the reduction—until the master would be willing to accept this reduced amount. I took it and put it into the bank. The master's lawyers made an effort to garnishee the money, but they failed. The bank wouldn't do a thing for them—an order had come down from Dublin telling the banker in Doneraile to keep the money until such time as it would be given back to me.

Things remained as they were for a half-year. The master was too cute for us, however. He didn't take any tenant to law. When he would be asked if he'd give the reduction, he'd never have any answer but that he was in no hurry for the rent, that he'd accept whatever amount would be given to him whenever any tenant would like to give it. You couldn't do anything with a man like that!

At last, the patience of some of the tenants was broken. They came to me and said that there was no good in leaving things as they were. There were some, they said, if the reduction itself was given to them, perhaps it wouldn't even be in their power to pay the remainder of the rent; they'd have to pay less, perhaps, without getting the reduction than if they'd got it!

I saw what their hurry was and I threw the money to them. I suppose they did better out of it than they would have done if they had got their reduction but had to pay up all they owed. There were a lot of them from outside Doneraile parish and so it wasn't easy to keep them combined and in one mind for any great length of time.

One good result came out of the whole business: a stop was put to the trick which used to be played on 'Sean Thingummy' and the 'moneyed-man'. And from this out, the moneyed-man was forced to find some other use for his money as he couldn't put it into Sean Thingummy's farm. If he were to use it that way any more, 'Grabber!' would be howled out after him! And it'd be better for him to run out of the locality than to have *that* howl going out on him! He was now forced to do what was good for him, even though it was against his will.

CHAPTER XXIII

MITCHELSTOWN

DURING the war in Doneraile between the tenants and the land-owners, a report reached us of another war over in Mitchelstown. A court sat in the town. There were two magistrates on the bench, a man by the name of Eaton, R.M., and Captain Stokes, R.M. There was a crown solicitor and Edward Carson was his name—Sir Edward Carson[1] he's called now, in this year of our Lord 1912. But he is the same Carson who was a crown solicitor there in 1887. The twenty-five years, which have since gone by, haven't made any improvement on him. The reason the court sat was to try William O'Brien, M.P., and John Mandeville[2] because of some public speech they were accused of and which was, according to the government of the time, against the law.

Although O'Brien and Mandeville had received an order to come and stand trial, each of them ignored the order. they didn't come to the court. If they didn't come, however, others came and it wasn't to court they came! They were in Mitchelstown to give to understand that they themselves and the entire public were in anger and fury because of the injustice which was to be done in the court that day when people were to be accused of breaking the law because they spoke in favour of right and against injustice.

Many people from Doneraile went to Mitchelstown that day. I myself went along with them. When we reached the town, we didn't see many people. Those who had reached the place before us were gone out of the town on the Limerick road to meet the people coming from that direction, so that they could march along with them back into the town. We were a good while waiting for them at the door of the house of Father Thomas Morrisson.

There's a fine, long, extensive space from the house, in which the priest was living, to the north and to the south and eastwards down to the main road of the town. We were waiting, looking down over the houses of the town, and instead of us having any expectation of a row starting up, it's how we were afraid that we would have only a very small gathering.

At last we saw the crowd coming. I recall that I saw John Dillon,[3] sitting in a carriage, among them. As soon as he came in sight of the big square where the meeting was to be, he lifted his head and

looked all around. The entire square was empty. I was looking at
him and I think he was disappointed. But as the crowd was coming
in, they marched up in the direction of the priest's house. Then the
place began to fill up. In a while, there was a good gathering of
people there, so that we were almost satisfied. There were two or
three long cars left out in front of the priest's house so that the
speakers would be able to stand up on them and talk to the
gathering.

A lot of gentlemen had come over from England. They came
exactly as we all had come, to give to understand that they
abhorred the manner in which the laws were being put into force in
Ireland. Henry Labouchère, M.P. was there, and John Brunner,
M.P., Thomas Ellis, M.P., and others besides them; some ladies
had come over from England as well, among them Miss Mander.
There were editorial staff from the big papers yonder, among them
Fred Higginbotham, and Bennett Burleigh, and John McDonnell
of the *Daily News*.

Fr Bartholemew McCarthy, D.D., was in the chair, and the
gentleman who were going to make speeches were on the long cars
outside the door of Fr Thomas Morrisson's house. As soon as the
crowd saw that the speeches were to begin, they pressed in around
the long cars. People who were there and who were familiar with
these things say that there were about eight thousand people
collected in around the carriages. If they were, twenty thousand
would have found room in the square without any doubt. I myself
was on one of the carriages and I had a good view of all who were
there and of the open space which was round about outside of
them. I didn't see as much as one single 'peeler' in any place on the
green, nor down on the street.

The speeching was only just starting when I noticed some
disturbance down over at the edge of the crowd. There were about
twenty peelers with a man for taking notes among them, and they
trying to take him along with them up to the place in which the
speeching was to be done. There was nothing to stop them from
going around, and it wasn't a great roundabout, to the north or to
the south of the people. They hadn't got a chance, at any event, of
bringing him with them through the middle of the people, for these
were packed together too tightly. Instead of going around, however, it's how they pushed their way into the people. The people
were trying to make room for them, but that was failing them and
no wonder. Then, when the people wouldn't do the impossible, the
peelers lifted their batons and struck them. But if they did, the

majority of the people had ashplants and, when they were struck they struck back in return. The peelers fled on the spot, themselves and the notetaker. I thought we would have calm then, but it wasn't calm that was coming. At the end of about five minutes, there came ten and forty of the peelers and each man of them with his gun. Up to then, there had been many men on horseback outside of the people who were on foot. When they saw the extra peelers coming with their guns, around with them until they made up a strong, solid cavalry between the people and the peelers. The peelers hadn't got a hope then of bringing the notetaker with them up to the chair. There was about three score of them there and they had no other business except to bring that man up with them.

If they had gone around, they would have had him up without any delay and, what is more, we would have made way for him on the spot. Nobody was stopping him. In place of that, it's how they reckoned on bringing him with them up between the cavalry and the people. They set about beating the horses. If they did, the riders turned the hind feet of the horses to them and they pressed the horses back in amongst them. The peelers raised their guns and they struck both horses and riders with them. The riders turned on them and struck them as well as they were able with whatever weapons came to hand. They made the work hot for about five minutes before the peelers fled out of the place. Some of the people followed in pursuit of them. Then the peelers went into the barracks from them. Every single thing was grand and quiet then. I was standing on the carriage, certain that we would have no further disturbance. It wasn't long until I heard, good and strong and forcibly, a shot from the barracks. I was amazed. There was neither fight nor trouble going on. What was their reason for the shot when no enemy was challenging them? The second bullet came. John Dillon leaped down from the carriage and away with himself and Fr Patrick O'Callaghan towards the barracks. I heard the third shot. As far as my memory goes back, I heard only the three shots. It was told to me afterwards that John Dillon and the priest went up to the window in the top of the house, where the peeler was on one knee and he shooting and loading, and that John caught him and tore him back from the window. When the people discovered that there were three dead, they scattered. The foreign gentlewomen went into the priest's house.

I was told that there were some soldiers in the town and that, when they heard the shooting, they came out. Whoever was in command of them saw at once that there was no sense to the shooting. He made a cordon of the soldiers that he had and, with the people on one side of the cordon and the peelers on the other, he kept them out from each other. If it had not been for that, the peelers would have killed more. They themselves and their officers were clean out of their minds. One of these officers was that same Captain Plunkett who had received, beyond in Youghal, some little time before that, the order from Dublin, 'Don't hesitate to shoot.' No wonder he had a fancy for shooting!

I heard afterwards that something occurred that day which greatly astonished the foreign gentleman, Henry Labouchère. He had a rug, which was of very dear fur, in his own carriage. When the crowd was scattering and everything mixed up, Labouchère was sure he would never again see his fine rug. He came to where the carriage was. He found the rug there before him, without anything having happened it but for a few people looking and wondering at it, saying to themselves that it would be difficult for any cold to go in through it.

'Indeed!' said Labouchère, 'if it had been over in London, or in any other place in the world, that such a thing happened to me, I would have very little hope of seeing my rug again! I say now, and I will say it from now on: the Irish are the most honest people in the world'.

To try the pair, William O'Brien and John Mandeville, was the reason the court sat that day. Neither of the pair had answered the call, and no wonder. The court set out a warrant for their capture and arrest. They were caught and put into prison. When the time came for it, they were brought to the same court in Mitchelstown for their trial, *mar dheadh*. I say *'mar dheadh'* because I was myself at the court and saw the 'trial' and certainly it was nothing if not a *'mar dheadh* trial'. The case was called. William O'Brien was the prisoner that day. A witness was called against him. The peeler, who had taken notes of his speech, was the witness against him. He told his story. He showed the little paper on which he had written the notes. Timothy Harrington[4] was the solicitor who was defending O'Brien.

'Let me look at that paper,' said Timothy.

The paper was handed to him. He looked at it sharply. Then he looked at the witness sharply.

'This is not the paper on which you first took the notes,' said he.

'They are the notes I took,' the witness said.

'Give me the paper on which you first took the notes,' said

Timothy. The poor witness stopped and he looked at the crown solicitor and up at the bench.

'You are not compelled to give him the notes,' said the crown solicitor.

'The case will not proceed another step,' Timothy said, 'until you give the other paper to me.'

The argument continued for a time. In the end, the poor witness had to put his hand in his pocket and take out his wallet, and to draw the old paper from the wallet and hand it across to Timothy. Timothy took the old, half-broken paper and he looked at it and read it. He let a little laugh out of him as he showed the paper to O'Brien. O'Brien let out a good strong laugh. What put them laughing? Here's what: the paper was after going to Dublin and coming back, and there was the order from the Chief Secretary in Dublin written across it, *'Not to be used'*. Look at that! An order from Dublin not to make any use against O'Brien of the notes that were taken of his speech when the speech was coming from his mouth, but to make use against him of those other notes which were put together after that! There's law for you! In exactly that manner, the law of England was being put into force in Ireland each and every day from that in Mitchelstown back all the way to when Black Thomas Wentworth put the law of England into force against the nobles of Connacht, and back farther again to the first day that the law of England came into the island of Éire.

* * *

I think that anyone, who would reflect on it, would realise that no more horrible, more disgusting, more unnecessary killing of people was ever done than that in Mitchelstown. it was exactly the same as if they had headed for a fair, or a Mass congregation, and began shooting the people without rhyme or reason. If they had gone around, where the way was empty, they would have been able to get the notetaker on one of the long cars as soon as any of the speakers went up on them. If a message had been sent to the chairman, asking that the notetaker be allowed up there, we would all have made room for him on the spot, and no wonder. What reason had we for making speeches but that our speeches would get to the ears of the government? In any case, permission had only to be asked for and permission was there to be had.

When I was in Charleville, at exactly the time of the first alarms of battle between tenants and landowners, a report was sent to me that there was to be a great meeting of tenants west in Tullylease and asking me to go there. I went. There was a grand meeting. When the business was beginning and the speakers going up on the platform, I myself went up on it. Who should I see, shoulder to shoulder with me on the platform, but the notetaker. Permission had been asked for him and received, and he was up there and nobody interfering with him.

We had a priest in the chair, Father Matthew McMahon, parish priest of Boherboy, a place which is about six or seven miles west of Kanturk.

Father James O'Moore, who was coadjutor at that time in Tullylease, had charge of the day's work and he was well worthy of it. He's parish priest here beside me now, in Rathcormack, and he's a Canon. He put everybody into his own place and the speeching proceeded, according to plan. The chairman made his speech. Father James made his and a well-judged speech he made. It was no harm to leave the business to him.

The time came for me to make my speech. I knew that the people listening to me had Gaelic well at that time, and, so that I would have a bit of fun at the expense of the notetaker at my shoulder, I began making my speech in Gaelic. All the people's eyes let up with fun on the spot. I noticed everybody giving me and the notetaker every second look. Jeremiah was his name, Jeremiah Stringer. I proceeded for a while until all the people were chuckling. Then I turned and I looked at Jeremiah. He was standing there with his pencil in his mouth. I stayed looking at him and I laughing, until all the people were waiting to see what I would say, and then I turned to them, 'I'm not saying,' said I, 'that Jerry isn't flummixed.' I wasn't able to say any more, there rose such a roar of laughter.

We did our business and had neither shooting nor killing. Father James (who is Canon now) gave us a grand, generous dinner. A lot of talk was done at the dinner, also. Some of the talk was angry, quite angry. But Father James had such self-possession, and prudence was so firmly rooted in him, that he used always take the edge from the anger before any harm could be done.

If the work had been done in Mitchelstown that day the way it was done in Tullylease about seven years before that, and the way it was done in a lot of other places as time went on, there would have been neither shooting nor killing there.

NOTES TO CHAPTER XXIII

1. Baron Edward Carson (1854–1935), the man who successfully took on the British government, when Home Rule for all-Ireland had been determined on, and was mainly responsible for the separate existence of the six counties of the North as a self-governing area, subordinate to the control of the British parliament. Paradoxically enough, he was born in Dublin, an Anglo-Irish Protestant. In the year of the Mitchelstown murders described by Canon O'Leary, he was counsel to the Irish Attorney General. He tackled the job of enforcing the 1887 Crimes Act with an almost rabid zeal. He was both a brilliant and unscrupulous advocate and got very many convictions for agrarian 'outrages'. He became an M.P. in 1892 and began his attacks on the Home Rule proposals of the time. Head of the Irish Unionists in 1910, he was instrumental in founding the Ulster Volunteers, in running guns from Germany and later in setting up a provisional government—with the wholesale support of the Conservative party. It was about this period *Mo Scéal Féin* was being written, with Carson the hero of the Orange Order and the the greatest mob-orator Ireland had seen since the hey-day of Daniel O'Connell.

2. William O'Brien (1852–1928), a Mallow man, became editor of *United Ireland* in 1881 at the height of the Land War and was so forceful in supporting the Land League and Parnell that the paper was suppressed. He was gaoled in Kilmainham with Parnell, where he put the 'No Rent Manifesto' in motion. An M.P. in 1883, three years later he and John Dillon launched the Plan of Campaign—'No reduction, no rent!' He was gaoled again under the terms of the 1887 Coercion Act—the year of the Mitchelstown murders. He tried hard to prevent discord when Parnell fell from grace and later formed the United Irish League to help restore unity (Canon O'Leary assisted him from the public platform in this work). He supported the Wyndham Land Act, formed the All-for-Ireland League but supported conscription and was thus swept aside in the tide of Sinn Féin.

John Mandeville (1849–1888), known as 'Fenian Mandeville', was one of those unselfish men who, though fortune had smiled on their birth, choose to support their less fortunate fellows. Active in the Land War, he died the year following the Mitchelstown 'trial'. Mitchelstown commemorates him (and the three men—Casey, Lonergan and Shinnick—shot by the police at the Land League meeting) with a monument in the Square.

3. John Dillon, who played such a big part in the political movements from 1880 onwards, was the son of the great Young Irelander and later M.P., John Blake Dillon. John junior was elected M.P. for his father's constituency in 1880, after he had accompanied Parnell on his American tour. Under the Coercion Acts, he was imprisoned several times. He and William O'Brien launched the 'Plan of Campaign' in 1886. He became leader of the anti-Parnellite group in the House of Commons following the 'split', succeeded Redmond as leader of the Nationalist Party which was swept aside by Sinn Féin. His son, James, became leader of the Fine Gael Party.

4. Timothy Harrington was one of the most extraordinary men in the period. Called to the Bar in 1887, he had founded a newspaper before becoming secretary of the Land League. When that was suppressed, he became secretary of the National League under Parnell's leadership. He, too, was in Kilmainham gaol with Parnell and is credited with the originating of the 'Plan of Campaign'.

CHAPTER XXIV

FROM DONERAILE TO CASTLELYONS

WHILE I was in Doneraile, I used to take an interest in the Gaelic language, but there wasn't much I was able to do. I used to speak it to anyone who would speak it to me, and I used read it out of any book, which had some kind of Gaelic in it, when I came across it. I had a name for Gaelic, at any rate, and now and again, questions used be coming through the post to me to solve.

A letter came to me one day from a lady[1] who was married to a son, or to a grandson, of Daniel O'Connell. She was a daughter of Bianconi, that man who used have all the coaches on the roads until the trains put an end to them. In the letter, she told me she had a manuscript which she had found down in Co Limerick, and that it was a manuscript of the keen which Eveleen O'Connell made on the death of Art O'Leary, when he was shot on the river-bank at Carriganimmy. She said that a certain man below in Co Limerick was attempting to translate the manuscript to English for her, but that she was afraid he hadn't enough Gaelic to do the work correctly. She asked me if I would have any objection to her sending the manuscript on to me for translation. Immediately, I sent an answer to her telling her that I had none and that I'd do the work as well as I could. She sent me the manuscript. There was a letter with it to tell me that there was one line the man had failed completely to make out; she said that there was a mention of some 'Madam Anne' in the line and that the man couldn't for the world make out who this 'Madam Anne' was.

'It is clear,' she wrote, 'that Eveleen laid the entire blame for the death of Art on this Madam Anne. I would like to find out, if this were possible, who she was and what she did against Art, or was Eveleen jealous of her.'

In English, she wrote the letter, of course, and that is the substance of the letter's contents. She told me where I would get the line in the manuscript. I searched and found it, and also the two lines before it. Here they are:

Art ua Laoghaire
Atá anso traochta
Ó mhaidin anné agam.

I admit that I opened my mouth and let a shout of laughter, which was heard in every part of the house, when I saw what a wicked woman—the evil-minded, malevolent Madam Anne!—had risen before me out of that tiny, little, unsuspected phrase *'O mhaidin anné*—'since yesterday morning'! It wasn't on the lady, who wrote the letter to me, that I laid the reproach, of course, but on the man below who was letting on that he understood Gaelic.

I sent the right meaning to her. I told her I had never heard any mention of Eveleen O'Connell having any jealousy for any 'Madam Anne' or for any other kind of 'Madam'.

Then I wrote out the entire lament in English as accurately as I was able, and I sent it to her. Of course, it wasn't with the elegance of the English I was concerned when I was doing the work, but the elegance of the Gaelic—and with how I would bring with me into English the elegance of the Gaelic and the strength of the Gaelic, and the vigour of the Gaelic, and the passion and rushing of blood that this Gaelic used put in my own heart when I used speak it aloud. I sent my English script off to the lady, with the Gaelic one she had sent me. I don't think my English pleased her at all. With the help of the English I had given her, she herself wrote another English version. But I would feel that she took the elegance of the Gaelic from the work altogether.

Like this, look: in the place where Eveleen would say *'Mo ghrádh go daingean tú!',* the lady would put English on it like this: 'Beloved of my steadfast heart!'[2] I could find neither taste, elegance nor grace in that. I suppose, however, it was fine for English—I heard knowledgeable people praise it.

*　　*　　*

While in Doneraile, I had an attack of sickness which very nearly took me from this world. I had been in full strength the day before—it came on me very suddenly, just as if poison were given to a person. I was in bed for two or three weeks. Then, it was the will of God that I got over it. In the town at the time, there was a good, knowledgeable doctor—one of the Riordans—and he took good care of me. The blessing of God on his soul, he's dead now.

I couldn't understand how I came to have the attack and I so strong and so healthy just before that; later on, however, I well understood it. The Awbeg River runs along from Buttevant to Doneraile and comes under a bridge to the north below the town. It's a dirty, little river. Into it goes the filth of Buttevant town, the filth of all the country from there eastwards to Doneraile, and then the filth of Doneraile itself, so that the water couldn't possibly be otherwise but full of that poison. Our water facilities in Doneraile consisted of a boy and his ass and a tub within the ass-car, which drew water to their doors for people who would pay for it. He used to take the water out at the bridge, right where all the filth of the town was going into the river. The people in my house used to go and get drinking-water from a spring-water well a little way from the town, because we were afraid of the river-water. With things as they were, it was very difficult not to make a mistake at times and put river-water on the table for the drinking. However it happened, I'm certain that it was water from the river which gave me the sickness.

There was a parish priest in the town once, who realised the danger from the water and he'd often try to get the Poor Board to bring water from some spring-water well nearby into the town through pipes—but he failed. If this were done, the people of the neighbourhood would have to pay some little extra tax because of it. They wouldn't agree to that. 'The water, which was good enough for them before this, is good enough for them now,' they'd say.

The senseless people! They ought to have understood that if a bad sickness were to come into the town through using that water, it would spread throughout the countryside and the country people would pay dearly for their miserliness.

In the year of our Lord, 1890, making on for the end of the year, the word spread amongst us that the parish priest, who was here in Castlelyons, was going to die. He died in the end of the first month of the new year. The blessing of God on his soul! Then, on the tenth day of the second month of the new year, a thousand, eight hundred, four score and eleven, the Bishop sent me a letter telling me to go as parish priest to the parish of Castlelyons. I am here since then.

NOTES TO CHAPTER XXIV

1. This was Mrs Morgan John O'Connell, who wrote one of the most fascinating books about 'old Irish life at home and abroad, 1745–1833': *The Last Colonel of the Irish Brigade*. The Colonel in question was Count O'Connell, an uncle of the Liberator's. In this book, Mrs O'Connell has

given an account of the career of the outlawed Art O'Leary—a distant relation of the Canon's—and includes both the original and a translation of the famous keen composed by Art's widow (who was, incidentally, a sister of the Count's). This version of the keen was taken down from a keening-woman known as Norry Singleton about 1800; Canon O'Leary's version of nearly a century later contains a few extra lines and some minor differences in the 400 odd lines.

2. A recurring line in the keen which is virtually impossible to convey in English. As it is used here, there is no equivalent in English of the word *daingean*—another example of speech that is *gonta*. Frank O'Connor (in *Kings, Lords and Commons*) gives us the finest translation of the keen; wisely, he ignores *daingean* altogether and ejaculates 'My love and my delight'—far, far truer to the original than Mrs O'Connell's flowery Victorianism.

CHAPTER XXV

CHAMPIONING GAELIC

I SUPPOSE that I was two years here in Castlelyons when the Gaelic language undertaking began in earnest in Dublin.[1] I understood from what was being said and from the publicity which was in circulation that it had been decided to cultivate the living language which was in the mouths of the people. I well realized that, if it was to be done at all, this was the correct way. I had Eugene O'Curry's books and the Gaelic grammar which O'Donovan had written and I knew that books such as these were incapable of adding as much as one day extra to the life of the Gaelic language. I knew that these men had admitted that they sought for no more than to secure and preserve in books as much as they were able of the Gaelic language, so that, when the people would have stopped speaking it, at least this much would be on hand. O'Donovan and O'Curry saw that the language was going slowly but surely—and they well knew that their work was incapable of preventing this.

I am positive, however, that they didn't realize the damage in that loss. I think both they and many others, at the time and long after it, felt that its disappearance would be of great benefit; they had grave reasons for thinking so..

In Ireland at the time, the people who had nothing but Gaelic, had their minds pinioned where everyday business was concerned. For example, in any kind of legal affair, the man with English was able to turn black into white on them and they had no means of defending themselves. If they gave their own account in Gaelic, none would understand them—except, perhaps, the man who was planning to do them an injustice. They used to have interpreters, but, if the interpreter had accepted a bribe, how would things be with them then? From whatever way it was looked at, it could be seen that the man without English was in disastrous straits. That was what caused Daniel O'Connell to say that he thought it better that Gaelic would be seven miles beneath the water of the western ocean! Before his eyes, he had seen terrible injustices constantly being done to the Irish by England's man, while the Irishman would be powerless to say one word in his own defence except that which was not understood. Daniel O'Connell himself did great work defending the Gaeil from such injustice; and he realized that he would have been incapable of doing this except for the fact that he had English so well as to be able to fight the English-speaking crew through the medium of their own speech.

None thought of promoting the two languages side by side. It was generally felt that there was no danger that Irishmen would not have more than enough Gaelic, whatever way the world at large would take to English. There were only the thoughtful few, like O'Curry and O'Donovan, who noticed that Gaelic was disappearing. I myself did not notice that there was any danger of this until I went to Maynooth College and saw grown boys without a single word of it.[2]

Thinking people and those who studied the flux of time understood that Gaelic was going. Men in public affairs and those who championed the people against the English-speaking crew understood that, the sooner all the Irish were speaking English, it would be for the better. What no one understood was the fundamental damage which would be done to the Gaelic race if they lost the Gaelic tongue: that it would be the same to them as if they had lost their very nature. No one understood the mortal destruction which would have been made on the Gaelic mind when the language would be gone and there was no longer in Irish hearts or on Irish lips, from Donaghadee to Cape Clear, anything but broken English. What could the labours of O'Curry or of O'Donovan profit a man who had nothing in his mouth but broken English and nothing to think on in his heart but the thoughts that broken English could give him?

It seems that Daniel O'Connell reckoned that, if Gaelic were seven miles beneath the sea and English in the mouths of all Irishmen, that they would have English every bit as good as he himself had it. If so, he was mistaken. Without a doubt, broken English was plentiful in Ireland in his time, but in no way did it impoverish the minds of those who were speaking it. How could it when they had all the beautiful, noble and liberal richness of Gaelic still in their minds? That richness is now gone from those of the Irish people whose Gaelic has gone. There are some who have realized the pillage amongst them and they are now making an attempt to gather that richness to themselves once more. It is far easier to cast off than to regain richness.

If the two languages had been cultivated side by side from the time the Irish people had begun in earnest to speak English amongst themselves, the two languages would have assisted each other and given a strength and accuracy to each other which neither could have attained by themselves alone. That was not done, and the signs were on it. When the two tongues were mixed, without any cultivation being done on either of them, what happened was that many people were left floundering in both languages. That is what caused Jeremiah Moynihan to speak the well-known lines:

The people with least sense in Éire
Are those without English or Gaelic

But I heard news and rumours from Dublin to say that a band was to be founded to cultivate the Gaelic tongue and to keep it alive as a living speech on the lips of people. I was overjoyed to hear it. I heard, too, that it was a young priest in Maynooth who was at the bottom of the attempt.[3]

The years went by. There's no need for me to give an account here of the labours and the affairs of those years, but, perhaps, it'd be no harm for me to say one little word about the movement. When we were beginning, I saw that we had to build on the young people in provision for the future. While reflecting on that, I became fully aware of the fact that we had absolutely nothing at all in the form of a book to put into the hand of a child so as to teach him Gaelic. As a result, I decided to write a special book for our young people, a book whose language would be free from the faults which could be found with most of the language of the poets, a book with language which would suit our young people, which would appeal to them. Such was the reflection which set me to writing 'Séadna'.

The book pleased everyone, young and old. It was read to the old folk and it appealed to them—in it they heard (something they had never heard until then!) their own kind of language out of a book. And it appealed to the young people because there was a great similarity between the Gaelic, which was in the book, and the English on their own lips.

NOTES TO CHAPTER XXV

1. See Appendix 15.
2. At this time, the percentage of the population which was Irish-speaking in the area about Castlelyons was between 13% and 21%.
3. The 'young priest in Maynooth' was Fr Eugene O'Growney, a Meath-man who had heard Irish spoken around him as a child about the time of

the Fenian rebellion. As a clerical student, he had attempted to form an Irish-speaking club in Maynooth College but without much success. However, he did become well versed in the language while at college and was later appointed Professor of Irish there—the first the seminary had had for a long time. He was one of the founder members of the Gaelic League, became editor of the *Gaelic Journal* and gave all his spare time to promoting the re-Gaelicizing of the country. His book, *Simple Lessons in Irish,* was the best book of its kind ever published and thousands learned to speak Irish with its help. Overwork brought illness. In 1894, the *Gaelic Journal* announced the retirement of its editor 'owing to a slight indisposition'. He was forced to resign his commission in Maynooth and emigrate to California, where he died at the early age of 36. In September, 1903, his remains were brought back to Ireland. Canon O'Leary preached the oration in honour of the dead man in Cork, Patrick Pearse did so in Dublin. The remains of Fr O'Growney were re-interred in Maynooth.

CHAPTER XXVI

TRIBUTE TO OUR LABOURS

TIME went by. I kept up the work. Evidently, it was appreciated that I had done my share fairly well, something which was indicated in 1912 by an event which would never have occurred had it not been so. On 21 April, the authorities in Dublin granted the freedom of the city to myself and to Professor Kuno Meyer,[1] on account of all we had done for the sake of the Gaelic language. The tribute was bestowed on him because of the work he had done on Old Irish, and on me because of what I had done for the sake of the living Gaelic.

We both tendered our thanks to the city authorities. While expressing his gratitude, Dr Kuno Meter said something which gave us all to understand that it wasn't today nor yesterday that he first started to take an interest in Irish matters. After some preliminary words, speaking in English, he said something like this:

'My grandfather told me when I was a child over in the city of Hamburg that, as a lad he did meet with Napper Tandy and that sure enough Napper Tandy "took him by the hand". He told me this long before I heard any mention of the *"The Wearing of the Green"*.

That showed that Kuno Meyer, his father and grandfather had a great regard for Ireland and the Irish long before the Gaelic language business had begun.

When the people of Dublin had paid us this tribute, we went off to St Patrick's College, Maynooth, as we had been invited by the President of the college, that illustrious priest and professor of theology, Monsignor Mannix, who is now an archbishop over in Melbourne. He had invited three of us, Professor Kuno Meyer and Doctor Bergin[2] as well as myself and we travelled from Dublin in a motorcar.

After dinner, the St Columcille society assembled in the Great Hall and we all had a great discussion; Gaelic and everything to do with it, of course, was what we discussed.

In the course of this and throughout the evening, I was often mindful of a certain tomb in the little cemetery behind the college. There's a heavy iron coffin in that tomb and in it are laid the bones of a certain person, a priest. The coffin and its contents had been brought a great way from the western hemisphere, from Los Angeles, over thousands of miles of land and water, to be laid here in this tomb, where now it rests. The bones of Fr Eugene O'Growney are inside in the coffin. He himself is up amid the joys of heaven. That same night, he was looking down upon us and he was glad. He saw the work going ahead vigorously and indefatigably after all the years— the work which had broken his own strength and which rent soul from body in the prime of his years, the work for whose advance he would have spent three lives if he had them.

When the authorities in Cork heard what Dublin had done, they felt they ought to do something similar and they decided to give the freedom of Cork City to Dr Kuno Meyer and to myself. They appointed a day for it, and, by the luck of the world, wasn't it 15 September, St Finbarr's Day, the saint of Gougane, who is the patron of the city.

I never expected the sight I saw that day! When myself and Kuno Meyer came out of the train in Cork, there was a great throng of children there to welcome us. They sang us a song in Gaelic, which Osborn Bergin had composed for them. The Mayor and his carriage were there to bring us to the City Hall. Out before and behind us and on each side, we had an escort, armed and accoutred as in the time of Cuchulainn. When I saw them, I remembered a day I had been in Cork, thirty years before, when the land war was aflame. The Red Earl[3] came to Cork to throw us all into terror and to subjugate us. I watched him come out of the train. He had an armed escort waiting for him—to protect him from us, *mar dheadh!* I remembered the Red Earl when I looked and saw my own guard.

'By the deer,' said I in my own mind, 'I've a better guard today than he had that day!'

We proceeded through the city, over the main bridge, west to that great, wide street where the 'Yellow Horse' used to be long ago, east again and over across the other bridge to the City Hall. All along the way, the people, young and old, were crushed together on each side of us, cheering and clapping their hands as they welcomed us. When we entered the great hall, it was full of people, so full that it wasn't possible for any more to come in. We spoke there and were spoken to, and it was a heart-felt wonder for us both with what excellence the young boys spoke Gaelic to us.

I think it'd be no harm for me to stop here and say, as the storytellers used to say in Éire long ago:

Gonadh é sin mo sgéal-sa go nuige sin. And that is my tale up to now.

NOTES TO CHAPTER XXVI

1. The foundation of modern Irish scholarship may be said to have been laid in Germany by Zeuss, whose work was continued by scholars such as Windisch, Zimmer and Kuno Meyer. Meyer had studied Germanic and Celtic philology at Leipzig and, from 1895, was Professor of Teutonic Languages at University College, Liverpool. In the same year, he founded the *Zeitschrift für Celtische Philologie* and (with Whitley Stokes) the *Archiv für Celtische Lexikographie*. In 1903, he founded the School of Irish Learning in Dublin. He made many beautiful translations of early Irish poetry into English; his editions and translations include *The Vision of Mac Conglinne*. *Four Songs of Summer and Winter*, and *Ancient Irish Poetry*. He translated many texts and his influence on both the Anglo-Irish literary movement and the literary revival in the Irish language was great. He sympathized with and gave a certain standing to the Irish language movement, and was held in high esteem. He was given both the freedom of Dublin and Cork.
2. Dr Osborn Bergin, born in Cork, learned his Irish as a student and spent two years studying in Germany with the help of a travelling scholarship from Meyer's School of Irish Learning. In 1908, he was appointed Professor of Old Irish in University College, Dublin. He was one of the most pleasing of the first 'revival' poets and edited a number of important texts. He was given the freedom of Dublin with Meyer and O'Leary.
3. i.e. Earl Spencer, Vice-Regent 1882-1887.

APPENDIX

I

PLACENAMES

In the very first sentence of this translation, I met with the problem of place-names: 'Kinsale' to the English-speaking Irishman means far less than 'Ceann Sáile' does to a native-Irish speaker, steeped in the traditions of his 'hidden Ireland' culture. In the first paragraph, Canon O'Leary used the name 'Éire', which would have possessed for him a far greater wealth of meaning, association, symbolism than ever 'Ireland' can do for the English-speaker; as he says recalling the first time he realized that Irish was a dying language: 'I would almost have preferred to go to some foreign country, to spend and end my life there, than to be in Éire and it turning into a foreign country. In my opinion, it would not be Éire at all when there wouldn't be a word of Gaelic spoken in it.' Today we know that he was right: Ireland is not Éire.

Originally, I had decided on retaining the Irish forms of placenames in those parts of the book where Irish was commonly spoken in the times described or where the traditional associations in a name were relevant. However, I have been persuaded (against my better predilections but not against my better judgement) to follow normal custom and to use the anglicized versions (in general) and provide in this appendix the Gaelic originals and their meanings.

There is one point I would like to stress. The Irish-speaking peasant's attitude to his home-area is in direct contrast to his English-speaking descendant's. 'The warm attachment of the Irish peasant to the locality where he was born and brought up,' noted Lord Derby in 1845, 'will always make the best and most carefully conducted scheme of emigration a matter of painful sacrifice for the emigrant.' Only during the famine did he ever leave his home willingly, if sorrowfully. All too often, his English-speaking descendant, whose homeplace possesses no meaning for him, looks on it as something to escape from as soon as he is able. It is very much a matter of language. Reading Canon O'Leary's litanies of placenames, when recalling the days of his youth, one senses that for him there is enshrined in these the history, the myths, the longings, the hopes, the *raison d'être* of himself, his family, his *muintir*. But no translation can do justice to the poetry of placenames.

AHADALLANE. Canon O'Leary writes this as *Áth an Dalláin*, 'The Ford of the Blind Man,' but it is more likely that the original was *Achadh a' Ghalláin*, 'The Field of the Monumental Stone'. There is, indeed, a cromlech nearby; A *gallán*, however, normally refers to a single, upright block of stone (similar to the hoar-stones of England), which marks an ancient boundary or tomb. The word is often corrupted to *dallán*. There are a number of gallauns in the region.

ARDPATRICK. *Árd Phádraig*: 'St Patrick's Height'. A village inside the Limerick border, traditionally the site of a church founded by the saint. The remains of a round tower and church are still to be seen.

BAILE IDIR DHÁ ABHAINN: 'Townland between two Rivers'.

BALLYNAMONA. *Baile na móna*: 'Townland of the Bog'.

BALLYVOURNEY. *Baile Mhúirne*: 'Múirn's Townland'. Múirn was a girl's name meaning 'love'. In legend, it was the name of the mother of Fionn Mac Cumhail. The Annals of the Four Masters record Ballyvourney as a camping-place of O'Sullivan Beare on his famous retreat from Dunboy in 1602. There are a number of Irish-speakers to be found in the area and the visitor may be lucky enough to see women wearing the traditional hooded cloaks peculiar to the area. A 'Court of Poetry' still survives.

BARRAHAURIN. *Barr a' Chaorthainn*: 'Summit of the Mountain Ash'.

BAWNATANAKNOCK. *Bán a' tSean-Chnuic*: 'The Pasture of the Old Hill'.

BEENALACHT. *Beinn na Leacht*: 'Pinnacle of the Standing Stones'. As Canon O'Leary describes it, the huge stone circles are there. Gallauns are often found near stone circles and there are a number in this area. Indeed, Ahadallane is only a few miles away.

BOHERBOY. *Bóthar Buí*: 'The Yellow Road'. Most probably an ancient name from times when good roads were few. *Bóthar*, a road, takes its name from *bó*, a cow. The tenth-century Glossary of Cormac tells us that two cows could fit on a *bóthar*, 'one lengthwise, the other athwart, and their calves and yearlings fit on it along with them'.

CAHERDRINNY. *Cathair Droinne*: 'The Hump-backed Fort'. *Cathair*, which in general refers to the ancient circular mortarless stone forts found mostly in the south and west, is very common in placenames. The original caher is gone and a ruined castle now stands in its place.

CAHERINDUFF. *Cathairín Dubh*: 'The Little Black Fort'.

CARRIGANASS(EY). *Carraig an Easaigh*: 'The Rock of the Waterfall'.

CARRIGANIMMY. *Carraig an Ime*: 'The Rock of Butter'. In ancient times there was probably a large milking-spot in the vicinity. Here, in 1773, the High Sheriff of Cork and his soldiers shot Art O'Leary, then an outlaw, and a famous keen was composed. O'Leary was a distant relation of the Canon's but belonged to a much wealthier branch of the family. See Appendix 2.

CARRIGNAMADRY. *Carraig na Madraí*: 'The Rock of the Dog's.

CARRIGNACORA. *Carraig na Cora* is the normal modern Irish name; the last word, however, is more likely to have been *curra*, giving the meaning 'Rock of the Wier'. The usual name in English is Castle Masters. There were O'Leary's residing here for nearly three centuries. The site is close by Inchigeelagh.

CARRIGASTYRA. *Carraig a' Staighre*: 'The Rock of the Staircase'.

CHARLEVILLE. See RÁTH LUIRC.

CLONDROHID. *Cluain Droichid*: 'The Meadow (or Hermitage) of the Bridge'. The original bridge (where the modern one is now) spanned the

Rìver Lee at Carrigadrohid. The ruins of a MacCarthy castle, built in the thirteenth century, stand here on a sandstone island in the river. The castle had a stormy history. Here, in 1650, when the O'Learys were losing their lands, Boetius MacEgan, Catholic bishop of Ross, was hanged because he refused to induce the Confederate garrison to surrender the Cromwellian forces. The MacCarthys were overlords to the O'Learys.

CLYDAGH. *Claodach (Claedig)*: 'Stoney-banked River'.

CULLEN. *Cuileann Uí Chaoímh*: 'O'Keefe's Little Wood'.

CURRALEIGH. *Curra Léithe*: 'Wier of Greyness (Brightness?)'. There is a river at the foot of the mountain of this name; it is also possible that the initial word is *currach*, 'a moor', which would correspond better with the nearby Derryleigh.

DERRYLEIGH. *Doire Léithe*: '(Oak) Grove of Greyness (Brightness?)'.

DERRYNAMONA. *Doire na Móna*: 'Grove of the Bog'.

DERMOT AND GRAINNE'S BED. *Leaba Dhiarmada is Gráinne*: 'Bed (Grave) of Diarmuid and Gráinne'. Legend has it that this pair eloped. She was supposed to be the wife of Fionn Mac Cumhail, he a warrior nonpareil. In fact, he was the Apollo of an early Celtic race. The 'bed' or grave is a cromlech of note.

DONERAILE. *Dún ar Aill*: 'Fortress on a cliff'. The *dún* (a word which occurs in many placenames) was a fortified residence for kings and chieftains, generally built on a high, flat mound, surrounded by one or more earthen walls.

DROMATHANE. Possibly *Druim a' tSionaichín*: 'The Hill-ridge of the Little Fox'.

DUHALLOW. *Dúthaigh Ealla*: 'District of the Swan'. See MALLOW.

ÉIRE. The English word 'Erin' comes from the dative case, *Éirinn*. No one is quite sure what it originally meant. The ancient form was Ériu, but this only serves to add to the mystery. Some have seen in it a not very plausible connection with the Aryans, others connect it with an early Celtic race. Whatever the truth, no scientific explanation will give the same meaning to the name as legend has done. Éire was one of three beautiful queens at the time of the coming of the Milesians or Gael. She has come down to us in various guises and always great men have recognized her and thought her worth dying for. Just before the 1916 Rising, W. B. Yeats powerfully dramatized the idea in his *Cathleen Ní Houlihan*.

FERMOY. *Mainistir Fhear Muighe*: 'Abbey of the Plainsmen'.

FUNCHEON RIVER. From *fuinnseann*, 'Ash-tree'; Funcheon probably means something like 'the Ash-producing River'.

GLENDAV. *Gleann Dáimh*: 'Glen of the Stag'.

GORTNASKEHY. *Gort na Sceiche*: 'Field of the Whitethorn'. *Gort* refers to an enclosed, tilled field.

IVELEARY. *Ua* or *Ó* means a grandson in particular and 'a descendant' in general. The plural Uí may be applied to a tribe or *muintir* and the ablative plural Uíbh is used in territorial designations. *Uíbh Laoghaire* therefore refers to the territory of which the descendants of Laoghaire, the O'Learys, were the ancient proprietors.

KANTURK. *Ceann Toirc*: 'The Head (i.e. Hill) of the Boar'. An old strong-hold of the MacCarthys, who were paramount over the O'Leary's in olden times.

KEEL. *caol*: 'A Narrows'. Normally refers to a narrow river in a marshy area.

KILGOBNET. *Cill Ghobnatan*: 'Gobnet's Church'. Up until recently, Gobinet was still a common name for girls in the area around here and Ballyvourney. St Gobnet, patroness of the latter town, founded churches in both places in the sixth century.

KILLARNEY. *Cill Áirne*: 'Church of the Sloes'. The O'Leary associations with Killarney would not be primarily concerned with 'Heaven's Reflex'. Firstly, there would be the Lear-like figure of Aodhagan O Rathille blindly staggering about the roads in 1726 crying to the night that he would not beg for help until he was coffined. The great poet was buried in Muckross Abbey (the Irish Tourist Board guidebook doesn't spare it a thought!) and the whole area is associated with the colossus who sang of the destruction of the Gaelic families and who, in his person, became symbolic of that ruin. He it was who lamented the downfall of Diarmuid Ó Laoghaire, the Canon's ancestor, who had had a Big House between Carrigawadra and Kileen in the Killarney district.

KILMALLOCK. *Cill Mocheallóg*: 'Mocheallog's Church'. The site of a monastery founded by the saint in the seventh century. Its history was one of recurring warfare between Irish and English forces down to the Treaty of Limerick.

KILSHANNIG. *Cill Seanaigh*: 'SEANACH's Church'.

KILWORTH. *Cill Uird*: 'Church of the Order, i.e. Friars'.

KINSALE. *Ceann Sáile*: 'The Head of the Brine', the highest spot reached by the sea-tide in a river. The name strikes like a death-knell in Gaelic history, for it was here that the English forces under Mountjoy and Carew conquered Ireland in 1602. Hugh O'Neill, Hugh Roe O'Donnell and Hugh MacGuire were the Gaelic commanders in a battle about which the historians are still puzzled; the fact that the Irish forces ought to have been victors only added to the tragedy. It marked the end of the old Gaelic order. With the Spanish fleet which had been under siege in the town, a prominent O'Leary sailed away to become one of the first of the 'Wild Geese'.

KNOCKBOY. *Cnoc Buí*: 'Yellow Hill'.

KNOCKANERRIBUL. *Cnoc an Iorbaill*: 'Hill of the Trail', i.e. a hill which ends in a ridge similar to a tail.

LISCARRIGANE. *Lios Carracháin*: 'Fort of the Rough Ground'. Canon O'Leary recalled there was nothing in their farm but bad land.

MACROOM. *Mágh Cromtha*: 'The Sloping Plain'. In the sixteenth and seventeenth centuries, the castle Canon O'Leary recalls in Chapter 8 was the scene of much fierce fighting. The castle and town of Macroom were in the possession of Admiral Sir William Penn, father of the founder of Pennsylvania, at one time. The castle was, obviously, a symbol of the English conquest; round about Macroom, the area is studded with MacCarthy and O'Leary fortresses.

MALLOW. *Mágh Ealla*: 'Plain of the Swan'. The 'swan' is a river, which flows into the Blackwater. In Mallow was born Thomas Davis, one of the most influential of Irish patriots in the last century.

MULLAGHANISH. *Mullach an Ois*: 'The Hill of the Fawn'. *Mullach* means a conspicuous, rounded hill.

MULLAROE. *Mullach Rua*: 'Red Hill'.

MAULNAHORNA. *Meall na hEorna*: 'The Knoll of Barley'. *Meall* signifies a small, round, 'lump' of a hillock.

NADANULLER. *Nead an Fhiolair*: 'The Eagle's Nest'.

RATHCORMACK. *Ráth Chormaic*: 'Cormac's Fortified Residence'. The *Ráth* was a circular mound of earth on which houses were erected; they are extremely common. Here, a handful of years before Canon O'Leary's birth, nine men had been killed by military forces during the Tithe war. Fr Mathew Horgan, the curate, composed a lengthy keen for his parishioners and it was published in Cork with a full report of the inquest. Here, Canon O'Leary began his first Irish classes.

RÁTH LUIRC. The comparatively modern town of Charleville was built on an ancient site, the name of which means 'Fort of Lurc'. Seán Clárach Mac Domhnaill, celebrated Gaelic poet, teacher and scribe, lived and was buried here; up to his death about a century before Canon O'Leary was born, he was chief poet in the Court of Poetry which used to assemble in the town. O'Leary would have been familiar with his work. Indeed, the poet Wall, of whom the Canon tells an anecdote in Chapter 13, spent an evening with Mac Domhnaill which is still recalled in a *búrdún*.

REDCHAIR. *Bearna Dearg*: 'Red Gap'. The English name is a translation of the Irish but has become corrupt. It was originally Red Sheard—West English for 'gap'.

RYLANE. *Reidhleán*: A green for dancing and sports.

SKIBBEREEN. *Sciobairín*: 'Little Boat Harbour'. A town renowned in song and story.

TOGHER. *Tochar*: 'Causeway'. Before cultivation and drainage began on a large scale some 250 years ago, there was much bog and marsh throughout the country. The *tochar* crossed such areas and was made from alternate layers of trees, earth and stone.

TRALEE. *Tráigh Lí*. There are several plausible meanings suggested for the name, but the correct one is almost certainly 'The Strand of Lí (son of Dedad)'.

ULLANES. *Uladhcha*: 'Stone Altars'. Sometimes called 'Druids' Altars', these were ancient tombs. Paradoxically, a Christian cult became mixed with the pagan and in Canon O'Leary's day there was a 'pattern' or pilgrimage to the vicinity of a cromlech.

YELLOW FORD (*Béal an Átha Buidhe*) on the river Callan, a little north of Armagh. In 1598, Hugh O'Neill routed the British forces of Bagenal, killing over 2,000 men.

FAMILY NAMES

MUCH of what I have said about placenames at the beginning of Appendix I also holds good for family names and my treatment of them in this translation. Here I give the Irish forms of those names mentioned by Canon O'Leary in those parts of the book where Irish was commonly spoken in the times described and where people would have been better known in their day under the Irish form.

BERGIN. Ó hAimheirgín: descendant of Aimheirgín, the latter meaning 'wondrous birth'. An Offaly family.

BUCKLEY. Ó Buachalla: descendant of Buachaill (meaning 'boy'). One of the typical Cork names, never found outside the county until after the Cromwellian plantations.

CORKERY. Ó Corcra: descendant of (he who wears) purple. A very common Munster name.

CREEDON. Ó Críodáin: desc. of C. Another old and very common Munster name.

DAVITT. Mac Daibhéid: son of David. Perhaps it originated with the medieval Welsh settlers in Tirawley. Common in Mayo, where it is also anglicized to McDade.

DINEEN. Ó Duinnín: Desc. of D. (Meaning 'little brown person'). A Cork family, hereditary historians to the MacCarthys who continued with their literary tradition until the latter half of the eighteenth century. Canon O'Leary's contemporary, the great lexicographer, Fr Patrick Dinneen was proud to take up where his ancestors left off.

DUGGAN. Most probably Ó Dubhagáin: desc. of Dubhagán, which may have meant 'the black' or, perhaps, 'the melancholy'. The name is often anglicized to Doogan. The name, which is well-known still in North Cork, belonged to a family who were powerful there more than 800 years ago.

FREENEY. A Norman name, de la Freyne (of the ash-tree). The family settled in Co Kilkenny and rose to some prominence. The Gaelic forms of the name are de Fréin(e) and Fréiní.

HICKEY. Ó hÍcídhe: desc. of Iceadh ('healer'). Famous in their hereditary position as doctors to the O'Briens of Thomond, the family did not spread over Munster until comparatively late times.

LUCY. Ó Luasaigh, a name peculiar to Cork until recently, whose origin is a puzzle.

MACCARTHY. Mac Carthaigh: 'Son of Carthach'. Carthach was a very ancient name, signifying 'loving', which was found among the Continental Celts of Caesar's time. The family traces its long history back to a third-century king of Munster and for centuries they were the chief family of the province. Although wilting during the Norman invasion, they remained very powerful until the end of the eighteenth century. The Stewart kings of Britain were descended from this Munster royal family and this mostly accounts for the support the Irish gave to the Stewarts, especially to James II and Bonnie Prince Charlie. The MacCarthys were overlords to the O'Learys; Canon O'Leary would not have forgotten that in his dealings with his bishop (see Chapter 19).

MACHALE. *Mac hÉil*: son of Howel. A Connacht name which has been generally accepted as coming from the Welsh settlers of Tirawley in the twelfth century.

MOYNIHAN. *Ó Muinhneacháin*: desc. of M. ('Munsterman'). A name commonly found in south-west Munster.

MURRAY. *O Muirighthe*: desc. of Muireadhach ('Sea-lord'). Sometimes anglicized to Murrihy. Powerful in ancient times, this family was one of the earliest to lose its power.

O'BRIEN. *Ó Briain*: desc. of B. The Brian in question is of course none other than Brian Boru, the 'Emperor of the Irish' who turned back the Viking tide. The name is very common in Ireland and there have been many famous men proud to bear it.

O'CONNELL. *Ó Conaill*: desc. of Conall ('the Powerful'). Conall was a name also found in very ancient times among the British and Continental Celts. The family have been in Kerry for almost a thousand years, where they were powerful. Perhaps more than any other family they were associated with the Irish Brigades. The most famous member of the family was, of course, Daniel O'Connell the Liberator.

O'CURRY. *Ó Comhraidhe*: desc. of C. A little-known Clare family.

O'CALLAGHAN. *Ó Ceallacháin*: desc. of Ceallach ('the warlike'). This family were descended from the warrior-bishop, Ceallachan Chaisil, king of Munster in the tenth century. The Norman invasion pushed them back west of Mallow and to the Muskerry district. Like the O'Learys, they were brought low by the Cromwellian confiscations. It is interesting to see how, as Canon O'Leary tells us, the two families made a match.

O'DONNELL. *Ó Domhnaill*: desc. of Domhnal. A Donegal family, still very numerous in the north-west, who were for centuries very powerful in the area. A centuries-old conflict with their neighbours, the O'Neills, came to an end when Hugh Roe (Aodh Ruadh) O'Donnell, inaugurated as 'The O'Donnell' in 1592 and the hero of his clan for his courage, gallantry and high-mindedness, joined forces with the Earl of Tyrone against the common enemy. After nine years successful campaigning, the battle of Kinsale brought complete disaster. O'Donnell died in Spain—it is said from poison—while attempting to get aid from King Philip.

O'DONOVAN. *Ó Donnabháin*: desc. of Donndubhán ('the black-brown'). Originally, a north Munster family, they were driven in ancient times to Cork and held a position of power there until after the Treaty of Limerick. A branch of the family settled in Kilkenny, from whom was descended the great scholar, John O'Donovan, who was O'Curry's brother-in-law and helpmate.

O'GRIFFEY. *Ó Gríobhtha*: desc. of Griobhtha ('the griffin-like', i.e. a great warrior)' The name is most often anglicized to Griffin or Griffiths. The family originated from the Clare-Limerick basin and Gerald Griffen, novelist and poet of the last century, hailed from this area.

O'GROWNEY. *Ó Gramhna*: a corruption of *Mac Carrghamhna* ('son of Spear-calf') a very old Westmeath family. The name O'Growney is very uncommon; the usual anglicization is MacCaron. Fr Eugene O'Growney came from an area quite close to the ancient family seat.

O'LEARY. *Ó Laoghaire*: desc. of the calf-keeper. To this day, this very ancient family has been associated with Co Cork, and have given their name to a large area in west Cork—Iveleary. They originally held sway on the south-west coast but retreated before the Normans into the hill-country of Muskerry, where they became lords under the MacCarthys. Their principal residence was at Carrignacora (Castle Masters), near Inchageela. They were continually taking part in the wars against the English and suffered heavily in the Desmond Wars, Diarmuid O'Leary, chief of the family, being attainted as a result. They also took part in the Nine Years War, Mahoun Mac Donagh O'Leary fleeing to Spain with De Aquila after the battle of Kinsale. Following the flight of the earls, they were reduced still further though it was not until 1642, when Cnogher Merygagh O'Leary and many other relations were attainted at Youghal, that they had to leave Car-rignacora. Two years later, Donnell O'Leary, described as a 'gentleman', was a member of the Assembly of the Kilkenny Confederation. That war went against the combined Irish forces, as did the next, so that it was in 1696 that Aodhagan O Rathaille was to lament the fall of the house of Diarmuid O'Leary at Killeen, near Carrigawadra—a poem which, as Daniel Corkery was to remark in the *Hidden Ireland*, 'has been found "alive" on the lips of "illiterate" peasants in Kerry in our own days'. Canon O'Leary did not know why Diarmuid had to leave, but the cause was obvious—the O'Learys had sided with King James. Kedagh O'Leary was a lieutenant in that army; the name O'Leary crops up again and again in any list of Wild Geese.

Coming nearer to his own time, there were two famous O'Learys from West Muskerry whom Canon O'Leary did not mention. The first was Art O'Leary, gentleman, officer in the Austrian Service, outlawed through spite and shot by a posse in 1773. His wife, an aunt of Daniel O'Connell's composed the most famous keen in the Irish language for him. Less close in blood but of the same family was Máire Buí Ní Laoghaire, poetess, who composed a never-to-be-forgotten song on a tithe-war battle in Bally-vourney. Another Arthur O'Leary had been an outstanding Franciscan friar in the late penal era. One of the greatest of the Fenians was John O'Leary—but he was not from Cork.

O'NEILL. *O Néill*: desc. of Niall, i.e. Niall Glúndubh, a king of Ireland, who was killed fighting the Danes in the tenth century and whose name features in some still famous poems. The family were to become one of the most celebrated of all. The original family territory was Tyrone and this county has always been most associated with the name, although Derry and

Donegal also came under their sway at different periods. Henry VIII made Conn O'Neill Earl of Tyrone and the tudor era witnessed some of the greatest men in the family's history, Conn, Shane the Proud, Sir Phelim and the leader whom Canon O'Leary mentions, Hugh, known to history as 'The Great'.

Hugh (or Aodh) was reared in the English court and was confirmed by Queen Elizabeth in the title of Earl of Tyrone and in the possession of the 'clan' lands. He successfully steered a middle course in the troubled political sea of the time until he was actually forced into rebellion by the English in Ireland. With the assistance of Hugh Roe O'Donnell and Hugh Maguire, O'Neill was invincible in the north. The battle of the Yellow Ford referred to by O'Leary cost the foreigners 5,000 men. In 1601, however, the English having overrun Munster, O'Neill and his allies came to Kinsale from the north where he lost all in one disastrous battle: the end of the Gaelic order. Although pardoned by James I, by 1607 O'Neill found his predicament too unbearable and he and many others of the highest families of Ulster left for the Continent. Hugh died in Rome, a broken man, in 1616.

Owen Roe (or Eoghan Ruadh) O'Neill, his nephew, has been called the 'first Irishman', as he was the first leader who saw the anti-British elements in Ireland, not as 'Gaeil' and 'Gaill', but as 'Irish'. He was one of the bravest and noblest figures in our history. An experienced professional soldier with the Spanish army, he returned to Ireland to become the most important leader in the 'War of the Three Kingdoms'. He was the only Irish general who could have stopped Cromwell, but he died (it is said, of poison) while preparing for the encounter. His greatest victory—at Benburb—was an empty one for it could not be followed up.

O'SULLIVAN. *Ó Súilleabháin*: desc. of Súil-dubhán ('the blackeyed'). Another famous Munster family, closely related to both the MacCarthys and the O'Callaghans. The name is normally associated with Cork and Kerry where the family were numerous and powerful up until later confiscations. There have been many famous bearers of the name.

PURCELL. *Puirséil*: diminutive of *porc*, Old French for 'a pig'. The Normans brought the name to Ireland in the thirteenth century and the family remained powerful in Kilkenny for several centuries.

TOOHEY. *ÓTuathaigh*: desc. of Tuathach ('Lord'). A Connacht family which moved to Cork in late medieval times and now common in west Munster. It is more often anglicized in Cork to Tuohig or Twohig.

WALL. *de Bhál*: from *du Val* ('of the valley'). A Norman name, one of the earliest to be found in the country and prominent in several counties, Cork amongst them. They were on the losing Catholic side in the Desmond rebellion and their lands were confiscated.

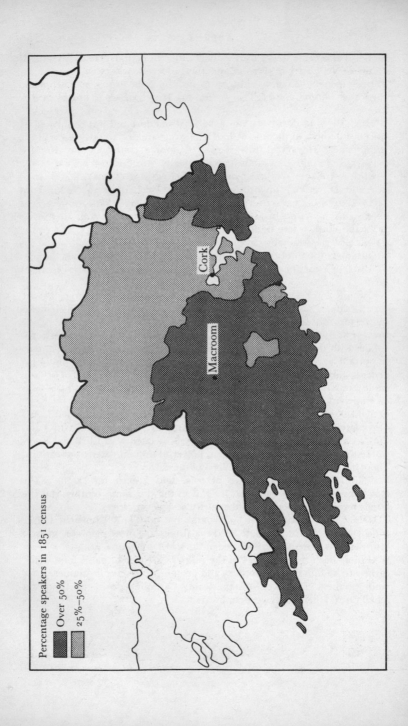

Percentage speakers in 1851 census

Over 50%

25%–50%

Cork

Macroom

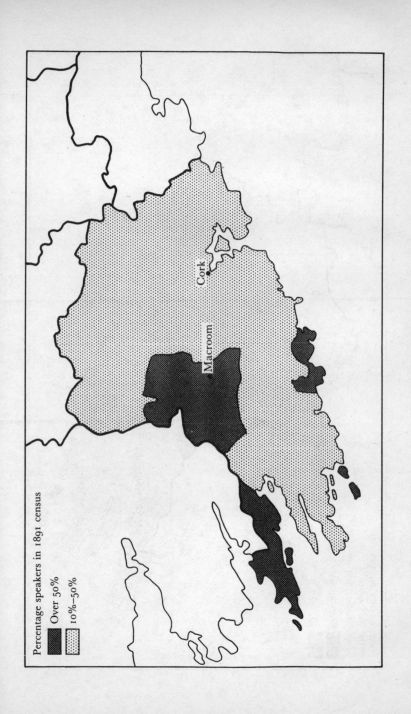

Percentage speakers in 1891 census

■ Over 50%

▦ 10%–50%

Cork

Macroom

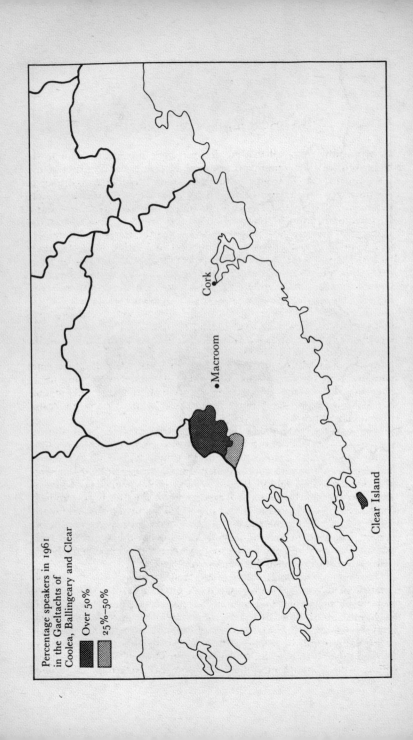

Percentage speakers in 1961
in the Gaeltachts of
Coolea, Ballingeary and Clear

Over 50%

25%–50%

Cork

Macroom

Clear Island

THE DECLINE OF IRISH IN CO CORK

IT is generally conceded that the greatest single immediate factor in the killing of Irish as the common language of the people was the great famine. It is estimated that, between 1846 and 1851, some 2½ million people died or emigrated; by far the greater majority of these were Irish-speakers, both monoglot and bilingual. The trend in emigration was to continue and is mirrored in the rapidly-decreasing numbers of Irish-speakers. In 1800, for at least 500 in every 1,000 Irish was the vernacular; immediately after the famine, in 1851, out of every 1,000 persons in Ireland, some 250 were Irish-speakers but the census returns for 1891 showed 850 out of every 1,000 who were unable to speak Irish at all! Today, after almost 50 years of self-government, it is doubtful if there are more than 30 persons per 1,000 whose home language is Irish. Emigration was not wholly responsible for this, of course—inferiority complex and social pressures, the conqueror's policy, education (not forgetting compulsory English in all its shapes and forms) and Anglo-Irish nationalism, utilitarianism and the attitude of the Roman Catholic Church, these were all important factors.

The character and personality of the people changed both rapidly and radically as a result. Nowhere has this been recognized with more poignancy than in the recent despairing admission of the indomitable guerilla leader of the war of independence, Dan Breen, that 'freedom came a hundred years too late'.

Cork was no different to any other area in which Irish was dying during this period—except that the rate was probably faster than in any other county. The statistical survey of the Royal Dublin Society in 1810 stated that, 'except in the towns, they seldom use any language but Irish, and even in some of the best cultivated districts most of the people can speak no other.' In the light of Canon O'Leary's note on English in his mother's family, it is interesting to find in this survey that 'in the wild and mountainous tracts, that divide the counties of Cork and Kerry, every bare-legged peasant converses fluently in English, while in the populous and well-cultivated country adjacent to the southern coast, the prevailing dialect is Irish.' Surprisingly enough, this pattern continued.

Contemporary accounts indicate that, immediately prior to the famine, upwards of 90% of the county was Irish-speaking. Canon O'Leary was twelve years of age when the census of 1851 was taken. This indicated that in his home area of West Muskerry some 75% of the people were Irish-speakers—although in Macroom 'English (was) used entirely by town people and generally in country parts of the parish, although there (were) a few who spoke Irish only'. In Duhallow, where Canon O'Leary spent some periods with relations, more than 40% were Irish-speaking; in Fermoy, where he went to college, some 35%. Irish was spoken by 12% of the inhabitants of Cork City; more than 50% of both city and county, comprising some 306,000 persons, spoke Irish as their vernacular.

By 1883, that figure had fallen to about 35%. In the parishes where Canon O'Leary acted as curate and finally as parish priest, the north-eastern part of the county, the language was dying rapidly. Probably Ráth Luirc (Charleville) area contained the highest proportion of Irish-speakers, especially on the Limerick side. The 1891 census gives these figures: Fermoy area (including Rathcormack and Castlelyons): 13%; Condons and Clangibbon (including Kilworth and Araglin): 20%. The Canon's home area, West Muskerry, still had 54% and Duhallow 25%. The county as a whole was about 31% Irish-speaking, some 120,000 people.

Four years after the formation of the Irish Free State (six after the death of Canon O'Leary), the census returns showed 22% Irish-speaking. Today, not a half-century later, there are perhaps 4,000 people in the county who can claim to be native speakers. Most of these belong to the now tiny West Muskerry Gaeltacht, which no longer has Canon O'Leary's birthplace within its borders. Twenty years ago, in his most informative book *Irish Dialects and Irish-speaking Districts*, Professor Brian Ó Cuív said that 'it is only in a few very restricted areas that Irish is still a native language (in Co Cork)—that is in parts of West Muskerry, of the Berehaven peninsula, of the coastal areas of Carbery, and in Ballymacoda.' But, by 1965, the compilers of the government white paper on the restoration of the Irish language could find only two Fíor-Ghaeltacht (truly Irish-speaking) districts in Cork: Muskerry (with 3,252 inhabitants) and Clear Island (235 inhabitants).

THE WRITINGS OF CANON O'LEARY

It was Eoin McNeill, one of the co-founders of the Gaelic League and later Chief of Staff of the Irish Volunteers, who really set An tAthair Peadar on his literary career. McNeill was editor of the *Gaelic Journal* at the time and wrote to O'Leary asking him to submit short-stories. O'Leary, probably spurred on by the publication of his letter to the Society for the Preservation of the Irish Language in 1878, had been getting into print occasionally in the columns of the *Irishman*. He first submitted a verse from folklore in 1893; McNeill had seen one of his short stories the following year. Now, these short stories would have little relation to those by O'Connor or O'Faolain, the short story as a conscious art form; O'Leary's were the *gearrscéalta* or droll, little tales countryfolk might tell around the fireside; such folktales are based on actual characters, the best of them are beautiful with an unconscious art while all of them are replete with social history. An tAthair' Peadar's *gearrscéalta* have been collected into volumes such as '*Ár nDóithin Araon*' (1919) and *Ag Séideadh agus ag Ithe* (1918). These small collections show An tAthair Peadar in a very attractive light.

When he began writing for McNeill in 1894, Canon O'Leary was fifty-five years old. In his remaining twenty-six years, he wrote, compiled, translated and adapted incessantly. Almost all his writings appeared first of all in journals and newspapers and later on (some 40 of them) came out in some kind or other of book form. He had immense influence, not so much because of what he actually achieved but because of the paths he explored and the lead he gave. He cannot be said to have been a great writer of imaginative literature; indeed, he produced very little really creative writing.

Séadna—based on a Muskerry version of an international folktale—is his *tour de force*. He began it in the *Gaelic Journal* in 1894 and it soon got recognition as the first important literary work to come out of the revival —'Literature at last!' exclaimed Patrick Pearse in delight. If opinion is still divided as regards the worth of *Séadna* as a whole, there is no doubt that much of the book is of great beauty. It indicated what could be done and paved the way for first-class writers such as O Conaire and Pearse himself. It weighed the scales very heavily in favour of *caint na ndaoine*, 'the speech of the people', as a literary medium and dealt a death blow to the then unhealthy and dangerous tendency to write in 'dead' Irish.

Niamh, a historical novel set in the time of Brian Boru and published in 1907, made an impact, too, though of nowhere near the same weight. It was not the first novel among the revivalists, but it was the first that was worthwhile reading. Like almost all O'Leary's work, it suffered from the unavoidable lack of critical proofing; publishers, like everyone else in the movement, were so glad to get material of the sort that no one dreamt of turning a friendly-critical eye on work which was not published as yet. Still, the book was a landmark in Irish language writing.

So too were his plays. The Canon knew nothing about the stage but wrote the first plays in the language. *Tadhg Saor* and *Bás Dallain* were issued in book-form in 1900; three others were written within the next half-dozen years. Though these initiated drama in Irish, there were only a few plays which were of even minor success until Brendan Behan's *An Giall* (in translation, *The Hostage*). On the other hand, O'Leary's *Mo Scéal Féin* began a vogue which at least led to the three Blasket 'classics'.

The Canon was celebrated for his rewriting in Modern Irish almost a dozen of the ancient king-stories ('sagas', if you will) and medieval tales, the best-known of which are *Bricriú* (1901), *An Craos-Deamhan* (1905), *Eisirt* (1909), *An Cleasaidhe* (1913), *Guaire* (1915). He was out of tune with them, withdrew the barbs from the anti-clerical satire of 'The Vision of Mac Con Glinne', bowdlerized the rowdy, randy sagas. It is to be regretted that An tAthair Peadar knew very little about literature. His modernizing of the histories, *Ceallachán Chaisil* (1907) and *Aodh Ruadh Ua Domhnaill* (1929), is much more of an objective success. Still, like everything else he touched, all these works added untold momentum to the literary revival in Irish.

His writings on Irish grammar and usage were, of course, of immense importance. Some titles: *Irish Prose Composition*; *Notes on Irish* Words and Usages; *Papers on Irish Idiom*. He was a good propagandist (especially in the columns of the *Leader*). Two collections—*Sgothbhualadh* (I, 1904; II, 1907) and *Comhairle Ár Leasa*—are of interest to the student of the times and their advice still holds good.

His translations read more like original works: somebody has remarked that he made Lucian's gods cavort like tinkers at a fair! The only thing Spanish about his *Don Quixote* is the name. An tAthair Peadar's method suited *Aesop's Fables* admirably, however, and this is a little mine of good things.

As might be expected, his religious writings were many. He translated the Bible, but by no means all of it has got into print yet. Among the religious works are: *The Four Gospels*; *Acts of the Apostles*; *Stories from the Holy Bible*; *Twenty-three Sermons*; *The Maccabees*. He compiled prayerbooks and a Catechism. Some of his best work is to be found in a beautiful translation of *The Imitation of Christ*. His final work was a life of Christ, *Críost Mac Dé*.

(Further information on the writings of An tAthair Peadar may be found in that invaluable compilation *Taighde i gComhair Stair Litríochta na Nua-Ghaeilge o 1882 anuas* by Muiris Ó Droighneáin (1936) and in *An tAthair Peadar Ó Laoghaire agus a Shaothar* by 'Maol Muire' (1939). In writing this book, both have been of great assistance to me.)

UPROOTING OF THE LORDS AND PROTECTORS

'Some foreign stranger'—to understand all that was entailed in this (for it was by no manner or means merely a change of lord) requires a knowledge of the relationship between the ruling families and the people. The chapter on 'The Big House' in Daniel Corkery's *The Hidden Ireland* gives us a particularly good insight into the situation; in fact, it uses as one example part of a lament for the fall of Diarmuid O'Leary's house at Killeen. The almost feudal system of the Gaelic order may not (though this is open to doubt) have been much better nor much worse than any other sort of feudalism, but it was infinitely better than the plantation system which took its place. So much worse was the latter, in fact, that it was easy to look back on the earlier period as something of a golden age. The 'foreign demons' and 'foreign boors', as they were often referred to in the poetry of the time, were ruthless business men and in no way considered themselves to have the duties of feudal lords. 'All our castles,' cried the great Gaelic poet, Dáibhí Ó Bruadair, 'are held by ill-bred upstarts, they are crowded with men of cheese and pottage.' It was not so much the change of lords which mattered, this was a common enough occurrance: it was the change of system, the absolute destruction of a social order.

Any study of the period, which does not include the social Gaelic poetry, is incomplete. For those who do not know Irish, I would recommend the first nine translations in the section, 'Peasants and Dreamers', in Frank O'Connor's *Kings, Lords and Commons*—as a starting point. Ó Bruadair and Aodhagán Ó Rathaille are the two great voices of the period. The absolute conquest of Ireland becomes symbolised in the fall of the great houses, the cutting of the woods, the end of the chase. What surprises Englishmen—and not a few Irishmen!—is the terrible contempt in which the British planters were held:

> Roughs formed from the dregs of each base trade, who range themselves snugly in the houses of the noblest chiefs, as proud and as exalted as if the sons of gentlemen. (J. C. MacErlain. *Poems of David O Bruadair.* Irish Texts Society, 1908.)

O Rathaille, addressing Ireland after the 'fall', prophesizes:

> Henceforth you shall be the drab for every withered crowd
> And every foreign boor shall have sucked your breasts.

The anonymous poet of *'Cill Chais'* sums up both the essence of the old order and the disaster that has overcome it in a few lines—in Frank O'Connor's translation:

And the great earls where are they?
The earls, the lady, the people
Beaten into the clay.

CANON O'LEARY'S ANCESTORS

The story of the Canon's branch of the O'Leary family is the story of Ireland in miniature. The *Uí Laoghaire* were one of the more ancient of families, being of pre-Goidelic origin and occupying the Corcra Laoighdhe territory in south-west Cork some 2,000 years ago. They held on after the Eoghannacht Conquest of Munster, but eight centuries later the upheavals caused by the Norman invasions removed them northwards to the West Muskerry area that has since borne their name, Iveleary, now the extensive parish of Inchigeelagh. Here, despite all the contemporary vicissitudes, they held sway in comparative security for some three centuries more.

We are most concerned with the proprietors of their second most important castle, at Carrignacora, near Inchigeelagh. First, in 1584, Diarmuid Óg saved his lands from confiscation by accepting a pardon, then his son, Tadhg Meirgeach, was attainted after the Nine Years War. Nevertheless, Tadhg's two sons remained in possession for a further forty years. Following Cromwell's victory and the great Plantation in the 1650s, sixteen O'Leary proprietors in all were outlawed and the lands again confiscated. The two sons of Tadhg Meirgeach, Diarmuid and Conor, were forced to leave Carrignacora Castle. The former removed to Carrignamadry, the latter to Cullen. Almost two centuries later, Canon O'Leary's father, a descendant of Diarmuid, married his mother, a descendant of Conor—peasants on a tenant farm 'with the grass of seven cows'.

In the meantime, the O'Learys had taken up arms yet again. In the War of 1688–91 one was a Major-General in King James's army, another a representative in the Kilkenny parliament. Following the Williamite victory, Dermod O'Leary became a rapparee chief and at least five others were similarly outlawed. Even so, several members of the family successfully claimed restoration of their estates. Carrignamadry Castle had been razed—a catastrophe lamented by the great poet Aogan O Rathaille—but the O'Learys again got possession of a remnant of their old lands. They finally had to leave in the mid-eighteenth century, possibly as a result of the last Jacobite endeavour. Both male heirs—one the Canon's grandfather—were saved from destitution by dowries of small farms at Liscarrigane.

Many members of this relatively unimportant sept attained prominence in the eighteenth and nineteenth centuries, including several high-ranking officers in various armies (among them Simon Bolivar's aide-de-camp), two Gaelic poets, a famous R.C. apologist, an outlaw whose death prompted the best-known lament in Gaelic literature, a Fenian leader immortalized in a Yeats poem, and a Gaelic author contemporaneous with the Canon.

THE WORKHOUSES

The much-vaunted 'Age of Reform' had a late start in Ireland but, while the changes which took place could hardly be termed as spectacular, there was much achieved by O'Connell which was solid and long-lasting. On 31 July, 1838, an act, which looked good on paper but turned out to be one of the most degrading in the statute book, received the royal assent: the Poor Relief act, which extended to Ireland the recently established English workhouse system. In practice, it was the most uncharitable system that could have been devised. These grim and forbidding poorhouses became the most hated and feared buildings in the country, although it was a bad time for the poor.

There had been 130 workhouses built throughout the country before the great famine. They were intended to relieve poverty, but this was in an age when the British property-owning classes considered that to be in need of charity at all was almost a criminal act. Within their walls, conditions were made so harsh that there were cases of people starving rather than enter them. What was even worse, virtually all public assistance ceased outside of these institutions with their advent.

Within a few years of their erection, however, the workhouses were overcrowded with famine victims. At the height of the famine, nearly 200,000 people were packed into houses intended for only half that amount. Typhus and relapsing fever were rampant. The death-rate was fantastically high. Many, with all hope for the future extinguished, went to the workhouses expecting at least a decent burial, but even this was denied to them. The diet in these institutions was not only worse than in the local gaol, rations were also smaller. In 1846, a Quaker philanthropist discovered that on the day of his visit to the Glenties workhouse there was not enough food to feed the inmates and that, on the day previous, they had had one bowl of meal and water!

Even after the famine, life in the workhouse was one of exceptional rigour. So hated was the system that, during the war of independence, some of them were burnt down.

THE NATIONAL SCHOOLS

The British government established this system of education in 1831. the national schools quickly began ousting the popular schools, the pay schools and hedge schools. What was even worse, they displaced the small classical schools throughout the country; for example, in Newtownstewart, Co Tyrone, where there used to be '20 teachers who have actually imparted classical instruction since the year 1800' in the parish, the 25 national schools gave 'no classical or superior education whatever'.

In many ways, however, there was a welcome improvement. For instance, the new system was the beginnings of free primary education at public expense. Also, teachers, received special training and had their salaries paid by the state. Schoolhouses were built. Quite a few of the miserably underpaid teachers educated remarkably well but, on the whole, any apprehensions that 'the National Schools would prove to be educational hotbeds for stimulating to an undue and morbid extent the intellects of (poor) children' soon vanished—unfortunately.

The schools played a major part in the decline of the Irish language and in the growth of the national inferiority complex. Twenty years after the first schools were founded, although Irish was still spoken by more than one-fourth of the population, all lessons were given in English and very harsh measures were taken to discourage the use of the language among the children. In 1901, the Gaelic League had its first successes in its campaign to re-introduce Irish onto the curriculum (see Peadar Ó hAnnrachain. *Fé Bhrat an Chonnartha*. Oifig an tSoláthair, Baile Átha Cliath, 1944). This was the beginning of a new era for the national school system; but, up until then, despite the name, there was nothing national about the education provided. The following verse, hung in every school, typified the general aim:

> I thank the goodness and the grace
> That on my birth have smiled,
> And made me in these Christian days
> A happy English child.

The Russians did not invent brain washing! No wonder Irish-speakers referred to these schools as 'Foreign Schools'.

'AGRARIAN OUTRAGES'

'With all this degree of courtesy, hospitality and cleverness amongst them,' wrote a land-agent shortly before the great famine, '(the Irish) are a very desperate people'. He was, of course, referring to the 'agrarian outrages' of the time, when the peasant took the law into his own hands. Such agrarian violence was then almost a century old, having begun during the reign of George III. It was directly caused by the pressure of tithes and rack-rents, hearth-taxes, forced labour and the Enclosure acts, by which the people were denied their ancient rights to commonages. There was a sudden growth, especially in Munster, of secret societies, called 'Whiteboys', 'Shanavests', 'Captain Rocks' and other local names. These societies inflicted terrible revenge on their enemies—on land agents, grabbers, informers. Arson, assassination, torture, maiming of animals—these were their methods. No effort was made to reform the atrociously bad land system; instead, the year 1765 saw the first of the coercion acts. These acts were re-introduced with regularity throughout the next century and a half—a proof that the country was in a continuous state of rebellion: it certainly makes one wonder at the narrow view of history contained in the 1916 Proclamation, which held that the Irish people had been in a state of armed insurrection *six* times in the previous three centuries.

The history of this 150 years of conflict is as yet almost unchronicled and all but ignored. Yet, it is as much the history of Ireland as Catholic Emancipation, Easter Week or Young Ireland and surely the importance of the Emmett rebellion of 1803 is that it was an urban expression of the rural movement. The secret combinations also came into the open in 1798, the Tithe War, the Famine rebellions and, of course, the Fenian rebellion. 1798 in Wexford was largely a 'Defender' movement blended politically with the United Irishmen and a glance at the columns of contemporary local newspapers show that the same held good for the rest of the country.

From its beginnings until the early days of the Land War of ninety years ago, the movement was largely Irish-speaking and was spurred on by the Gaelic poets. It is only in this, its proper light, that we can see the *raison d'être* of the so-called Jacobite poetry. A century and a half of Irish history needs to be re-written; it can only be determined so after a thorough investigation of Irish-language sources.

MAYNOOTH AND THE IRISH LANGUAGE

Obviously one of the greatest moments of his life (if we are to judge from the last chapter of *Mo Scéal Féin*) was when Canon O'Leary was welcomed back to Maynooth College by his former pupil, the future Archbishop Mannix, after he had received the freedom of Dublin on account of his labours for the Irish language. Canon O'Leary gave an address in Irish that night and proudly he noted that there was a great deal of Irish being spoken by those present. What a contrast to the attitude in those days when he was a student! Respect and affection for the language, however, did not wax for too long in the college, and we have had to wait until very recent years for what seems to be the beginning of a new wave of enthusiasm which will prove fruitful.

Maynooth has had a very chequered career as regards the language. Waves of enthusiasm have been repeatedly followed by waves of apathy, if not antagonism. Back in 1806, it was Dr John Lanigan, Professor of Hebrew and Holy Scripture, who was a prime mover in the foundation of the famous Gaelic Society. Some years earlier, a student, Paul O'Brien, was employed as a teacher of Irish; from his ordination in 1804 until his early death sixteen years later, he was Professor of Irish. This O'Brien was a native-speaker from Meath, a popular poet and a scholar. He continually pleaded the cause of the language with the church authorities and would seem to have been one of the first to argue that the language would act as a buffer against irreligion and materialism. Fr O'Brien, the first Professor of Irish in the college, died young and it was left to the young Professor of Theology, the future Bishop of Tuam, Dr John MacHale, to carry the banner. Within a handful of years, however, he was transferred to the west. From this period on, he was a lone voice in the wilderness, warning against the dangers of anglicization.

Under the influence of Daniel O'Connell ('I am sufficiently utilitarian not to regret the abandonment of Irish. A diversity of tongues is no benefit.'), the tide, which had looked as if it might be running in favour of the language, was now ebbing among the Maynooth-trained clergy. After all, it was the Age of Utilitarianism and most of the clergy, with the inferiority complexes of the class they were mostly drawn from, were not indifferent about being out of step.

Not only that but the period witnessed a wholesale effort to win the Irish peasantry over to the Established Church—through the medium of Irish. The attempt failed but struck a devastating blow at the language, for the Roman Catholic clergy panicked and urged their flocks to abandon the language in case it turned out to be the means of their destruction. The teaching and reading of Irish in those areas where proselytism was vigorous was forbidden, collections of manuscripts were made and burnt publicly and preachers fulminated against the language from the pulpit.

The survival of the language was not helped by the pro-British attitude of the hierarchy and of church leaders in general. Many ingenious and disarming arguments were produced to explain that such an attitude was both right and fitting, but the real reasons would seem to have been that the hierarchy were drawn from the better-off (and more complexed) Catholic classes and that this pro-British tendency was always rewarded by the system which gave the British government a negative veto on the appointments of bishops. Men of this cast of mind became further antagonistic towards the language after the government grew afraid of the national feelings which were being evoked by the researches of the Ordnance Survey team—time and the Gaelic League were to prove government fears well-founded.

Just before the advent of the great famine, the British government made a further effort to bind Maynooth to it with hoops of steel by trebling the annual grant to the seminary: they can not have been too displeased with the result.

There was at least one seminarian of this period, however, who did trojan work for the language—the future Canon Ulick Burke. While a student in the college, he was writing simple Irish lessons in the *Nation* and also produced an Irish grammar. Forty years later, he was an active member of both the Society for the Preservation of the Irish Language and of the Gaelic Union.

The census of 1851 indicates that there were about 200 of the students and staff of the college who had registered themselves as Irish-speakers, at most only 45%. Ten years later, as the young Peter O'Leary became too well aware, the figure must have been much less and the inferiority complex much greater. The advent of Fenianism only aggravated matters: one recalls immediately how Cardinal Cullen, horrified to discover that some of his clergy were attending Irish classes run by O'Donovan Rossa in the Mechanics Institute, hurriedly slapped a ban on them.

The same period witnessed the active spread of a new type of Catholicism—the type which has since, unfortunately, become to be accepted as 'Irish Catholicism'. This type, because it equated Victorian respectability with Christianity, fobbed off on the population a French Jansenism (in place of Gaelic joy) and Italian sentiment (in place of Gaelic emotion). A mortal blow was struck at Gaelic spirituality; it is probably true to say that a mortal blow was also struck at the Gaelic language.

It is true that, for a very short period, Maynooth College witnessed a fantastic change in attitudes within its walls. What brought this about is open to question—the optimist thinks of a natural reaction, the realist of a swan-song. In 1882, a student formed an Irish Society in the college. It didn't last too long but that youth was in time to become Maynooth's first Professor of Irish for quite a long period; his name was Eugene O'Growney. He was a founder-member of the Gaelic League and, within the eight years left to him in this life, set the country and his fellow clergy on fire. To attempt to summarise the work in the Gaelic Renaissance by the younger Maynooth-trained clergy in these few lines available to me would be not only futile but unworthy.

But, in the very first flush of success came catastrophe: on points arising from the Gaelic League's insistence on compulsory Irish in education, the President of Maynooth, Canon O'Leary's former pupil, Daniel Mannix, and the Professor of Irish, Dr O'Hickey joined bitter issue. Dr O'Hickey fled to Rome to plead his case: eight years later he was still in Rome and only returned home to die in the same year, 1917. Dr Mannix made a determined effort to cauterize the wound; the symbolical gesture came in the invitation to O'Leary, Meyer and Bergin to Maynooth after they had been made freemen of Dublin.

The wound did not heal. The best that can be said about the attitude of the Church authorities subsequently is that they have kept Gaelicism at arm's length. Dr Philbin of Clonfert recently stated that 'in its attitude to the language, the Church in Ireland merely reflects the outlook of the ordinary people of Ireland'. There is a great deal of truth in this, of course, but it does not explain, for instance, how seminaries such as Maynooth have turned out non-Irish-speaking priests who eventually found themselves ministering in Irish-speaking areas.

2 In conclusion, it must be noted that there is a resurgence in things Gaelic among the students of Maynooth.

THE CHURCH AND FENIANISM

In the Oireachtas lecture of 1967, Fr Tomás Ó Fiaich, Professor of History in Maynooth College, gave a detailed account of the complicated relationships between the Fenians and the bishops and clergy of the Roman Catholic Church; the text of that lecture, *Eaglaisigh agus Fíníní*, may be found in the columns of the Irish-language weekly, *Inniu,* issues of 20 and 27 October, 1967.

Perhaps the initial reason for the attitude taken by the Church leaders, as typified by Cardinal Cullen, lay in the débâcle which had brought the Tenant Right League of the early 'fifties to a disgraceful end. It will be recalled that some of its leading Catholic members, Keogh, Sadleir and the rest of the 'pope's brass band', sold out to the government and thus had advanced their own careers through the championship of Catholic interests. Many priests had played a big part in the League, which seemed guaranteed to gain great success until the treachery of the leaders. The people lost all trust in constitutional methods and turned once more to physical force methods, to Fenianism. In the despondency following the collapse of the League, Cardinal Cullen ordered his priests to refrain from taking an active part in politics from that on. Consequently, when the body of the Fenian, Terence Bellew MacManus, was brought from San Francisco to Dublin, no participation in the lying-in-state nor in the funeral processions was permitted. Four priests did attend the burial, however, one of them being Fr Patrick Lavelle, from Archbishop MacHale's diocese of Tuam. Fr Lavelle further publicised his sympathy and Cardinal Cullen immediately reported him to Rome. His Christmas pastoral letter, condemning the Fenians as they were a secret society and declaring them to be hostile to the faith, was the first of many.

Early in 1862, Lavelle was on the offensive, outlining the church's doctrines on the right of rebellion. The Synod of Bishops attempted to put Lavelle in his place but without the co-operation of Dr MacHale this was not possible. Redress from Rome had as little effect. In 1863, the recently-founded *Irish People,* the paper to which Canon O'Leary took so much exception, entered the fray. The *People* argued well—it was Charles Kickham of *Knocknagow* fame who was the main writer. The Polish revolution, which had had the approval of the ecclesiastical authorities, was cited as an example; so too was the request of the Irish bishops for volunteers to defend the Papal States against Garibaldi's attacks.

The result, however, was only to make Cullen more antagonistic towards the Fenians and he did everything in his power to get Rome to put its most powerful interdict into practice. But, for the time being, Rome and Britain were on unfriendly terms and the Fenians escaped excommunication.

But the ordinary clergy and the Fenians were drawing closer together. After all, it was the abhorred traitor, Billy Keogh, who had sentenced O'Donovan Rossa to penal servitude for life; and surely no self-respecting clergyman could range himself on Keogh's side, especially when (as the ballad-singers put it):

Lord Norbury of old was something in the style of him,
If you heard him slanging clergymen in Galway and Mayo,
But Norbury himself lacked the venom and the guile of him,
For neither he nor Jeffreys was a patch on Billy Keogh.

The British government were quick to notice the change and charged Rome with it. Shortly before the rising of '67, Bishop Moriarty of Kerry made his infamous statement that hell was neither hot enough nor deep enough for the Fenians. Cullen, realizing that it had been a bad move, was upset over this. In mitigation of Moriarty, it is often said that he was referring to American Fenians whom he believed did nothing but incite others to rebellion. Whatever the truth was, even his own priests turned against him, with good results for a Home Ruler some years later.

After the confusion of the rebellion, we find the priests almost as a whole throwing themselves into the movement to save the leaders from hanging. Cullen himself visited the Lord Lieutenant. Canon O'Leary mentions the effect the hanging of the Manchester Martyrs had on his colleagues; Dr Keane, O'Leary's bishop and one of the handful of pro-Fenian bishops, presided at a Requiem Mass. The old lion, MacHale, helped found a nation-wide collection for the dependants of the dead men. The character of the typical Fenian, which brought the clergy into sympathy with them, has been beautifully captured in Canon Sheehan's The Graves at Kilmorna (Phoenix, Dublin). The Canon gives his witness of the events of 1867, with great feeling and sympathy, in essays which may be found in Literary Life (Phoenix, Dublin).

In 1870, however, Cullen and the British government, whether working separately or hand-in-glove will perhaps never be known, made almost simultaneous representations to Rome to excommunicate the Fenians. This was done, but, as far as I know, the edict was never issued in either Tuam nor in Canon O'Leary's own diocese, Cloyne.

While Cullen's attitude can not be termed an about-face, it is surprising to find him pressing for excommunication at a time when he had seemed most sympathetic to the Fenian prisoners. The answer might, at least in part, be found in the interest Marx and Engels had been showing in the movement. Engels, it may be remembered, had given Mrs Jenny Marx the credit for the freeing of O'Donovan Rossa because of the publicity she had given the case in a French paper. Marx, too, had written on the subject and had had it discussed at a high level. There was as well the memory of the Fenian connection with the 1848 revolution in France. However (as I have pointed out elsewhere in this book) such ties were at most skin-deep.

(Recommended reading: Seamus Ó Coigligh. *Marx, Engels agus na Fíníní.*
A series of four articles in the Irish-language weekly, *Inniu,* beginning on 23
December, 1967; also T. W. Moody (Ed.). *The Fenian Movement.* Mercier
Press, Cork, 1968.)

THE SOCIETY FOR THE PRESERVATION OF THE IRISH LANGUAGE

In some mysterious way, this society had its roots in the Irish classes the Fenian, O'Donovan Rossa, had begun in Dublin more than ten years earlier. It came into being in 1876, when the literary and historical societies, the Ossianic and the earlier Irish Archaeological Society, had become inactive. It was the first organized effort to attempt to prevent the extinction of the Irish language. The names of the more active members of the society are now very well-known—men such as Dr Douglas Hyde, Dr Sigerson, Michael Cusack, Canon Ulick Burke, David Comyn, John Fleming, Fr John E. Nolan; Dr Croke was the group's patron.

There has long been a tendency to speak of the society and similar groups of the earlier period in a slightly derogatory manner; this is unfair. The 'Preservation' group—despite Canon O'Leary's opinion—did much good work and, if results are anything to go by, certainly justified its foundation. It published a series of useful primers and also good, cheap editions (with translations) of works like *Diarmuid and Gráinne, Children of Lir* and Keating's *History*. It secured recognition of Irish by the Intermediate Board of Education and could proudly point to the fact that 403 students had sat for the Intermediate Irish examination in 1891. It put the emphasis on saving Irish from extinction, initiated Irish-language columns in the newspapers. Most important of all, among its off-spring was the Gaelic League.

However, the more active members of the society were becoming increasingly dissatisfied and felt that the efforts made were not enough. These broke away in 1880 and formed the Gaelic Union. By 1882, the Union was publishing a periodical (a step which had been opposed in the older society), bilingual, scholarly and propagandist; this was the *Gaelic Journal,* with David Comyn as its first editor.

After adverse criticism from British sources and a snub from Archbishop McCabe, the *Union* became increasingly conservative and actually repudiated its desire to restore Irish. In disgust, a splinter group was formed to keep the Irish language spoken in Ireland: the Gaelic League, founded 1893.

CANON O'LEARY AND THE SOCIETY FOR THE PRESERVATION

OF THE IRISH LANGUAGE

Professor Brian Ó Cuív was, I believe, the first to realize that Canon O'Leary had become confused as regards his dealings with the society. (See: *Éigse. A Journal of Irish Studies*. National University of Ireland. Vol. IX, Part IV.). O'Leary had no letter published in the columns of the *Freeman's Journal* as he erroneously believed in 1913; the letter in question, written to the publishers (Gill and Son) of the primers prepared by the Society for the Preservation of the Irish Language, appeared in the *Irishman*, in May, 1878. Some little while before this, the society had prevailed on the editor to give them a regular column and they were obviously pleased to publish the letter 'not only for its correctness and style, but for the signs of progress which it reports for the Gaelic movement in the schools of (the Rathcormack) locality'. A translation of the letter was also given—so much for the absurd belief that the society couldn't read it!

Below, I give my own translation of the text:

Rathcormack, Co Cork.
30 March, 1878

Gentlemen,

I send to you a postal-order for five shillings and eight pence as payment for the twenty books I received from you.

You asked me if I had anything useful to say about Gaelic and this place to let you know.

Firstly: There are up to twenty people in our little school here and they come together every evening learning the lessons, and I myself teach them and I am able to say that they are going ahead nicely. There are more outside of this who, after beginning well, grew impatient and did not attend anymore. At the same time, I think some of them will return when they see the business going ahead and their colleagues speaking Gaelic. I have two or three who had never spoken a word of it until six months ago and they are now able to quote from memory and to understand this little rhyme:

'The wren we found down on the river-meadow
In the shelter of a rock and a silk cravat on him
We brought him to ye—may there be plenty in your house
And may ye be seven times better this time next year.'

Now I have a little thought to set before you. The work impressed this much on me. If an ordinary man over twenty years of age comes to me, who never before spoke a word of Gaelic and was not used to it, there isn't a chance of getting a word of it into his mouth; but if I set out to teach a child of ten years, he will learn it as fast as I speak it. Another thing, those people who know a little and are used to Gaelic have no respect for it, for they think it a sign of respectability to know nothing about it. If it were possible to get that out of their hearts, it wouldn't take very long for them to learn it and speak it nicely.

Now if Gaelic was being taught in the ordinary schools, there would be two things being done: the young folk would be learning it without realizing it and it would get home to the older folk that it was a great shame for them not to know it.

I would think that if you set about it you would be able to get the entire country in agreement to get that much from the law-makers; and then more Gaelic would be taught in one, single year than will be now learned in ten.

The writing-book you sent me came to hand safely. When the boys saw it, they very much wanted one. Please send me twenty others of the sort.

I am hoping that it won't be long until we have another small school here beside Knockennaboulary. I have promised a person from there that I would show him Book One and Book Two of the Irish primer. He will take home the two books and his people will see them and he says they will all make an effort to learn Gaelic. I will give them every encouragement and I don't think they'll have any trouble as they all use Gaelic in their ordinary conversation.

Asking God to prosper your work. Good luck,

I am, Peadar Ua Laoghaire.

Certainly no sign of crossed swords there! Nor, if we examine the books in question, is there any sign of the quotation regarding the burdening of the reader with 'the mysteries of Irish aspiration'! The following, however, does appear in Book One:

We hope our readers will not find fault with the seeming incongruity of some of the sentences given in the exercises, as it was very difficult to find suitable sentences without making use of Aspiration or Eclipsis which we wished to avoid in the first book.

However, in the first edition there were several mistakes as regards aspiration. These were corrected in the later editions and may have been the cause of the 'strike' Canon O'Leary mentions.

Still, where there is smoke there is fire and the Canon's remarks in chapter 16 and their general tone sound very like the dissents of those who broke away from Fr Nolan's society and formed the Gaelic Union.

The books in question had a fantastic sale. In the ten years after 1877, over 72,000 copies of Books One, Two and Three were sold. The growing interest in Irish may be gauged also from the fact that the first and second books of the Gaelic Union's Irish primer went to a total of 47 editions in 20 years. These books had their faults but they paved the way for Fr O'Growney's *Simple Lessons in Irish*.

THE GAELIC LEAGUE

Perhaps the best way to attempt to convey the impact of the Gaelic League in as short a space as this is to supply some pertinent quotations:

> The only body in Ireland which appears to realise the fact that Ireland has a past, has a history, has a literature, and the only body in Ireland which seeks to render the present a rational continuation of the past. (Douglas Hyde.)
> 'The most revolutionary influence that has ever come into Ireland.' (Patrick Pearse.)
> 'We only succeeded after we had begun to get back our Irish ways; after we had made a serious effort to speak our own language; after we had striven again to govern ourselves. We can only keep out the enemy and all other enemies by completing the task.... The biggest task will be the restoration of the language. (Michael Collins.)

The Gaelic League was founded with the exclusive aim of keeping the Irish language spoken in Ireland and re-creating Irish culture, but its philosophy had far-reaching effects. The immediate factors in the formation of the League were the splintering of the old Society for the Preservation of the Irish Language, David Comyn's successful attempt to found an Irish-language journal and the initiative of Fr Eugene O'Growney, Professor of Irish in Maynooth College and editor of that journal. On the 31 July, 1893, after Fr O'Growney had contacted those interested, nine men met to attempt the impossible and the Gaelic League was formed. Besides O'Growney, the most important of these were Douglas Hyde (later Ireland's first President) and Eoin MacNeill. The process of 'de-Anglicization' was begun almost immediately. Rapidly, the public imagination was caught and the national conscience awakened. D. P. Moran vigorously propagated Hyde's gospel in his paper, the *Leader* (Canon Peter O'Leary was one of his chief contributors), and the movement for an 'Irish Ireland' was accelerated. In 1898, there were 58 branches throughout the country, two years later there were 120, in 1902 412, in 1904 593. The United States and Argentina provided huge sums of money. The League was both educational and social with its language, history, drama groups and its dances, feiseanna and annual oireachtas (a cultural and literary festival, perhaps its most influential contribution to Irish life at the present time). From 1898, it had its own bi-lingual weekly newspaper and published thousands of copies of books and pamphlets. With the goodwill of the greater majority of the country, it brought into education the system known as 'compulsory Irish' and also founded Gaelic Colleges for training teachers—in the year previous to the Easter Rising, there were 19 of these. In fact, as Horace Plunkett, founder of the agricultural co-operative movement, wrote, the League was invigorating every depart-ment of Irish life and adding to the intellectual, social and moral im-provement of the people.

The moral improvement was very marked—and vindicated the aims of the publicists. Circumstances had forced a low type of politics on the people in the Parnellite and post-Parnellite period; the rabble of Sheehan's *The Graves at Kilmorna* was no figment of the imagination. The inspiration of the League brought a more ennobling spirit, one re-miniscent of and re-creating that of pure Fenianism. It was an idealist's inspiration, linking the traditions of such men as Davis and Tone as well as the Fenians with traditional Gaelic nationalism. Hyde and the others caused a mental revolution and restored self-respect and self-reliance—the connection with Arthur Griffith's *Sinn Féin* is obvious. One aspect of the League is too often forgotten: its promotion of local industry. It's *Sinn Féin* attitudes were an encouragement and, among other things, the 'Buy Irish' campaign stems from this period. (Indeed, it is significant that the only section of the population which did not re-quire the urging of the 'Buy Irish' campaign of the last few years con-stitutes the language revival movement.)

The League never claimed to be a political movement but the national memories and spirit it evoked made it, as Pearse recognized, a great revolutionary influence. Collins, as we have noted, felt it was indispensable for the future of the nation. But, since then, the League has lost headway, even direction. The Easter Rising and the War of Independence swept away many of its greatest figures. The losses not only continued in the Civil War but, even worse, that period replaced national idealism with national disillusion. A new (and not unexpected) attitude was to grow up among the remaining faithful in the years after order had come to the Free State: that the work of the League was done, the native government would safeguard the language, Irish had been 'saved'. The ensuing years have proved them terribly wrong.

Canon O'Leary was among the first supporters the League had drawn to itself. He became a figurehead, 'a little god to us all' and, outside of his literary contributions, was a most enthusiastic worker 'in the field'. He became Vice-President of the movement after Fr O'Growney's premature death, but had disassociated himself from it by 1917.

Recommended reading:

Donal McCartney. *From Parnell to Pearse* in *The Course of Irish History*. Mercier Press, Cork, 1967.

Tomás Ó hAilín. *Irish Revival Movements* in *A View of the Irish Language*. Stationary Office, Dublin, 1969.

Donall Ó Corcora. *What's this about the Gaelic League?* Connradh na Gaeilge, Áth Cliath, 1942.

Dubhghlas de hÍde. *Mise agus an Connradh*. Foillseacháin Rialtais, Áth Cliath, 1937.

Daniel Corkery. *The Fortunes of the Irish Language*. Irish Life and Culture Series, The Mercier Press: Cork, 1969.

Peadar Ó hAnnracháin. *Fé Bhrat an Chonnartha*. Oifig an tSoláthair, Áth Cliath, 1944.

PROJECT-BIBLIOGRAPHY

Mo Scéal Féin, with its related backgrounds and significances, lends itself particularly well to forming the fulcrum for a study-project. This bibliography, which contains all the books I have consulted while working on this book, has been compiled with that end in mind.

HISTORY AND BIOGRAPHY:

T. W. Moody & F. X. Martin (Ed). *The Course of Irish History*. Mercier Press, Cork, 1967.

Edmund Curtis. *A History of Ireland*. Methuen, London, 1961.

Mrs Morgan John O'Connell. *The Last Colonel of the Irish Brigade: Count O'Connell and old Irish life at home and abroad, 1745–1833*. (in two vols.) Keegan Paul, Trench, Trübner, London, 1892.

Sean O'Faolain. *King of the Beggars*. Nelson, London, 1938.

Cecil Woodham-Smith. *The Great Hunger*. Hamish Hamilton, London, 1962.

T. W. Moody (Ed.) *The Fenian Movement*. Mercier Press, Cork, 1968.

D. Mac Uidhir & An Bráthair Peadar. *Fir 1867*. Cló Grianréime, Áth Cliath, 1967.

'Maol Muire'. *An tAthair Peadar Ó Laoghaire agus a Shaothar*. Brún & Ó Nualláin, Áth Cliath.

F. Sheehy-Skeffington. *Michael Davitt*. MacGibbon & Kee, London, 1967.

R. Barry O'Brien. *The Life of Charles Stewart Parnell*. Nelson, London, 1911.

Michael Davitt. *The Fall of Feudalism in Ireland*. Harper, New York, 1904.

Conor Cruise O'Brien (Ed.). *The Shaping of Modern Ireland*. Routledge and Keegan Paul, London, 1960.

A. M. Sullivan. *Old Ireland: Reminiscences of an Irish K.C.* Thornton Butterworth, London, 1927.

F. S. L. Lyons. *John Dillon*. Routledge Keegan Paul, London, 1968.

Walter McDonald. *Reminiscences of a Maynooth Professor*. Mercier Press, Cork, 1967.

N. Brennan. *Dr. Mannix*. Angus & Robertson, London, 1965.

F. O'Connor. *The Big Fellow: Michael Collins and the Irish Revolution*. Clonmore and Reynolds, Dublin, 1965.

Micheal O'Suilleabhain. *Where Mountainy Men have sown*. Anvil Books, Tralee, 1965.

Rebel Cork's Fighting Story. Anvil Books, Tralee.

Dudley Edwards, Desmond Williams (Ed.). *The Great Famine. Studies in Irish History 1845–52*. Irish Committee of Historical Sciences. Browne & Nolan, Dublin.

FOLKWAYS:

Daniel Corkery. *The Hidden Ireland*. Gill, Dublin, 1924.

Rev. M. McGrath, S. J. *Cinnlae Amhlaoibh Uí Shúileabháin: The Diary of Humphrey O'Sullivan*. (Intro., Trans., Notes.). Irish Texts Society, Dublin, 1931.

Kevin Danaher. *In Ireland Long Ago*. Mercier Press, Cork, 1962.

Kevin Danaher. *Irish Country People*. Mercier Press, Cork, 1966.

Domhnall Bán Ó Céileachair. *Scéal Mo Bheatha*. An Gúm, Áth Cliath, 1940.

Peadar Ó hAnnracháin. *Fé Bhrat an Chonnartha*. Oifig an tSoláthair, Áth Cliath, 1944.

R. B. McDowell (Ed.). *Social Life in Ireland. 1800–1845*. Cultural Relations Committee of Ireland, 1957.

W. R. Le Fanu. *Seventy Years of Irish Life*. Arnold, London, 1893.

Séamus Ó Duilearga (Eag.). *Leabhar Sheáin Í Chonaill*. Brün & Ó Nualláin, Áth Cliath, 1964.

Conrad M. Arensberg. *The Irish Countryman: An Anthropological Study*. MacMillan, London, 1937.

E. E. Evans. *Irish Folkways*. Routledge & Keegan Paul, London, 1967.

Eric Cross. *The Tailor and Ansty*. Mercier Press, Cork. 1970 Edition.

Robert Gibbings. *Sweet Cork of Thee*. Dent, London, 1949.

Robert Gibbings. *Lovely is the Lee*. Dent, London, 1951.

CULTURE:

Douglas Hyde. *Literary History of Ireland from the earliest times to the present day*. Ernest Benn, London, 1967.

Robin Flower. *The Irish Tradition*. Clarendon Press, Oxford, 1948.

Daniel Corkery. *The Fortunes of the Irish Language*. Irish Life and Culture Series, The Mercier Press, Cork.

P. H. Pearse. *The Murder Machine* in *Political Writings and Speeches*. Talbot Press, Dublin, 1962.

Muiris Ó Droighneáin. *Taighde i gComhair Stair Litríochta na Nua-Ghaeilge ó 1882 anuas*. Foillseacháin Rialtais, Áth Cliath, 1936.

Seán de Fréine. *Saoirse gan Só*. Foilseacháin Náisiúnta, Áth Cliath, 1960.

Diarmuid Ó Laoghaire, S.J. *Our Mass, Our Life: Some Irish Traditions and Prayers*. Irish Messenger Office, Dublin, 1968.

LÁNGUAGE

David Greene. *The Irish Language (An Ghaeilge)*. Cultural Relations Committee of Ireland, 1966.

Brian O Cuív (Ed.). *A View of the Irish Language*. Oifig an tSoláthair, Áth Cliath, 1969.

Brian Ó Cuív. *Irish Dialects and Irish-speaking Districts*. Dublin Institute for Advanced Studies, 1951.

H. Goad. *Language in History*. Penguin, Middlesex, 1958.

Simeon Potter. *Language in the Modern World*. Penguin, Middlesex, 1960.
Simeon Potter. *Our Language*. Penguin, Middlesex, 1950.
R. Graves & A. Hodge. *The Reader over your Shoulder*. Cape, London, 1947.

FICTION

Canon Sheehan. *My New Curate*. Phoenix, Dublin.
Canon Sheehan. *The Graves at Kilmorna*. Phoenix, Dublin.
Canon Sheehan. *Glenanaar*. Phoenix, Dublin.
Canon Sheehan. *Literary Life: Essays and Poems*. Phoenix, Dublin.
E. Somerville & M. Ross. *The Irish R. M. Complete*. Faber & Faber, London, 1962.
Myles na gCopaleen. *An Béal Bocht*. Cló Dolmen, Ath Cliath, 1964.
Daniel Corkery. *A Munster Twilight*. Mercier Press, Cork, 1963.
Frank O'Connor. *The Stories of Frank O'Connor*. Hamish Hamilton, London, 1953.

POETRY

Thomas F. O'Rahilly. *Búrdúin Bheaga: Pithy Irish Quatrains*. Browne & Nolan, Dublin, 1925.
Seán Ó Tuama. *Caoineadh Airt Uí Laoghaire*. An Clóchomhar, Áth Cliath, 1961.
Frank O'Connor, *Kings, Lords & Commons*. MacMillan, London, 1962.
J. C. MacErlean, S.J. *Poems of David O'Bruadair. Vols. I, II, III*. Irish Texts Society, Dublin, 1908, 1911, 1916.
Rev. P. S. Dinneen & Prof Tadhg Ó Donnchadha. *Dánta Aodhagáin Uí Rathaille (New Edition of the Poems of Egan O'Rahilly)*. Irish Texts Society, Dublin, 1909.
Dáibhí Mac Conmara. *Aogán Ó Rathaille: Dánta*. Aquila, Áth Cliath, 1969.
An tAth Doncha Ó Donnchú. *Filíocht Mháire Bhuí Ní Laoghaire*. Foillseacháin Rialtais, Áth Cliath.

WORKS OF REFERENCE AND OTHER SOURCES

Edward Mac Lysaght. *Irish Families: their names, arms and origins*. Hodges Figgis, Dublin, 1957.
Rev Patrick Wolfe. *Sloinnte Gaedheal is Gall: Irish names and surnames*. Gill, Dublin, 1923.
P. W. Joyce, *Irish Names of Places*. Gill, Dublin, & Longmans Green, London, 1913.
Dubhghlas de hÍde. *Mise agus an Connradh*. Foillseacháin Rialtais, Áth Cliath, 1937.
Dónal Ó Corcora. *What's this about the Gaelic League?* Connradh na Gaeilge, Áth Cliath, 1942.
J. W. Boyle (Ed.). *Leaders and Workers*. Mercier Press, Cork.
J. J. Horgan. *From Parnell to Pearse*. Browne and Nolan, Dublin, 1948.

Éigse. A Journal of Irish Studies. Vol. IX, Part IV. Brian Ó Cuív. *Litir ón Athair Peadar Ua Laoghaire*.

Inniu. Four articles beginning 23 December 1967. Séamas Ó Coigligh. *Marx, Engels agus na Fíníní*.

Inniu. Two articles beginning 20 October 1967. An tAth Tomás Ó Fiaich. *Leacht an Oireachtais: Eaglaisigh agus Fíníní*.

Canon O'Leary. *Ár nDóithín Araon*. Browne & Nolan, Dublin.

Canon O'Leary. *Ag Séideadh agus ag Ithe*. Browne & Nolan, Dublin.

An tAth Peadar Ua Laoghaire. *Sgothbhualadh*. Brún agus Ó Nóláin, Áth Cliath.

An tAth Peadar Ua Laoghaire, Can. *Mo Sgéal Féin*. Brún agus Ó Nualláin, Áth Cliath.